SEXUAL
UNDERSTANDING
BEFORE
MARRIAGE

D1531634

SEXUAL UNDERSTANDING BEFORE MARRIAGE

HERBERT J. MILES

Introduction by Dr. Paul Popenoe,
founder and president of the
American Institute of Family Relations.

PYRANEE
BOOKS

Zondervan Publishing House
Grand Rapids, Michigan

Dedicated to
DOROTHY WILSON MILES
My Wife
whose high Christian and moral ideals
have inspired me
through the years

SEXUAL UNDERSTANDING BEFORE MARRIAGE
Copyright © 1971 by Zondervan Publishing House

Pyranee Books are published by Zondervan
Publishing House, 1415 Lake Drive, S.E.,
Grand Rapids, Michigan 49506

Library of Congress Catalog Card Number 76-146559

ISBN 0-310-29212-3 (mass market)
ISBN 0-310-29231-X (trade paper)

Quotes from *The New Testament in Modern English* by J. B.
Phillips, © 1957 by The Macmillan Co. Used by permission.

Printed in the United States of America

86 87 88 89 90 91 / ZO / 26 25 24 23 22 21

TABLE OF CONTENTS

Introduction

Preface

1. Some Honest Questions Youth Are Asking
   About Sex 17

2. Understanding Your Parents and Your Present
   Ideas About Sex 27

3. Reproductive and Sexual Organs 34

4. Why Society Objects to Premarital Sex Relations 48

5. Necking, Petting, and "Making Out" on
   Social Dates and During Courtship 60

6. Some Questions About Sex Examined 70
   *1. Are some women sexually frigid? 2. Is the male
   more sexual than the female? 3. Does a woman's
   body shape affect her sexual capacity? 4. Is sex just
   a game? 5. Is sex as normal as breathing, eating, and
   drinking? 6. Does following Christian principles and
   living a consecrated Christian life block good sex
   life in marriage? 7. Has Christianity always opposed
   sex? 8. Do primitive people have any moral codes?
   9. Do right and wrong change from time to time
   and place to place? 10. Does the new morality
   make our past sex traditions out of date?*

7. Other Pertinent Questions About Sex Discussed 102
   *1. Why is sexual intercourse evil before marriage
   and good after marriage? 2. What is the difference
   between an engaged couple three months to three*

weeks before marriage and the same couple after marriage? 3. Does sexual control before marriage cause dangerous psychological repressions that will destroy normal sex life and personality in marriage? 4. Why is it necessary to have rules and regulations? 5. How can youth know where to draw the line between right and wrong? 6. Who should draw the line, the boy or the girl? 7. Is the desire to marry a virgin a legitimate concern in marriage plans? 8. Should a couple feel guilty if they by accident go all the way? 9. Should an engaged couple confess previous sexual experiences to each other before marriage? 10. Is it wrong for an engaged couple to look forward anxiously to their sex life in marriage?

8. How to Control Sex Until Marriage 102

9. A Program of Sexual Control for Young Men:
   A Study of Masturbation 137

10. A Healthy Sexual Identity for Young Women:
    A Distinction Between Reproduction and
    Sexuality and a Study of Female Masturbation . 163

11. Dealing With Past Sexual Sins 178

12. Some Practical Christian Guidelines for Sexual
    Control From Puberty Until Marriage 189

APPENDIXES

I. The Biblical Case for Premarital Chastity 199

II. Hebrew-Christian Ontology as Related to
    Sex Morals 210

III. Some Suggestions to Churches on Sex Education 214

IV. A Selected Bibliography 218

INTRODUCTION

If there is national confusion about the place of sex in life today, it is largely because the great, sound majority of the population has allowed a noisy, ill-informed, and radical minority to do most of the talking. It is past time for those concerned about the American home to go over to the offensive and give the public the facts, identify plainly the issues at stake, and demand recognition of the basic principles on which civilization has been built, and on the maintenance of which it must survive. This book by sociologist Herbert J. Miles provides valuable ammunition for the campaign. It ought to find wide use in the Christian community.

The church has stood for correct policies; but my students—intelligent and earnest men and women—complain that it has not done enough to put those policies effectively into the hands of everyone who needs them. Interestingly, they speak of the doctrine of Love—central to Christianity if anything is!—as one which particularly needs clarification and emphasis, since the word is so persistently and flagrantly misused. Dr. Miles leaves no doubt in the mind of any reader about the damaging distortions which the word suffers twenty-four hours a day!

The appendix, in which the author details ways for the church to "implement" its teaching, is of far-reaching value. I am afraid his estimate of the number of parents who give their youth correct sex education is based on a selected group at a church-related college and can not be matched in the bulk of the population. For instance, the U. S. Public Health Service estimates that there are two new infections with venereal disease *every minute,* and the director of Los Angeles County Venereal Disease Control reported recently that "only 3 per cent of parents prepare their children adequately to handle this problem." Similarly, in the case of the 800 babies born out of wedlock *every day,* it is found that an enormous majority of the young people involved have had from father or mother no real understanding of "what it's all about."

One of this book's practical suggestions is that church women form classes in which they can learn how to talk to their own offspring! Merely hearing the sound of their own voices is a good beginning. The men of the church should certainly follow this pattern, for a close relationship between a father and his sons and daughters is necessary and, in the case of the boys, is the main preventive of the development of homosexuality.

Every youth group may well make topics and discussions on sexual understanding a regular part of its program. An outside speaker, carefully chosen, could lead the discussion every few months. It would be a poverty-stricken organization indeed that could not afford to allow ten dollars from its yearly budget to buy a copy of Dr. Miles' book and a dozen or so inexpensive pamphlets that could be circulated outside as well as in the group. To make the lesson more concrete, a committee, preferably made up of both sexes, might visit the divorce court and report what is really happening. Another committee might visit the marriage license bureau and learn what requirements the county makes of those about to wed; and if they could cap this off by witnessing the marriage of a couple by a justice of the peace, my guess is that they would have a vivid recognition of the desirability of a wedding ceremony carried out under religious auspices, either in church or home.

One of the real difficulties hampering sound preparation for marriage and family living is that the young people of the church have not received, and learned to use effectively, the material that will enable them to challenge "permissive" arguments on the spot and to refute them successfully by pointing out convincingly the fallacies and untruths on which they are based. Dr. Miles' book will give them the ammunition.

The church should lose no more time in extending its war on the spread of sexual laxity and the deterioration of family life. It should throw all its great resources into this war. Books like this one are indeed timely.

Paul Popenoe, Sc.D.
Founder and President of the
American Institute of Family Relations
Los Angeles, California

PREFACE

What are the four most important social influences in human culture? The replies to this question may be many and varied. In my judgment the correct replies are as follows:

1. First, *Christianity* is the most important social influence in existence. The reader may ask, "What kind of Christianity?" In reply, I refer to both the general and specific principles of the Scriptures: the kind of Christianity that was believed and lived out in the lives of the prophets of the Old Testament and the disciples and followers of Jesus in the New Testament; the Christianity believed and practiced by Luther, Calvin, Zwingli, and the leaders of the Protestant Reformation; the kind of Christianity that inspired and led in movements that developed the great evangelical groups in America. All of this is applied Christianity as it produces faithful consecration and courageous action in the lives of individuals; this type of Christianity zealously endeavors to uplift the individual, the community, and the social groups and organizations that bind them together. This is the most significant social influence in existence.

2. The second most important social influence is the *organized human family,* including father, mother, and through reproduction their sons and daughters. Permanent monogamous marriage characterized by responsi-

bility, fidelity, love, and tenderness is civilization's second most prized asset.

3. The third most important social influence is *human sexuality* when it is lived out between husband and wife in the "one-flesh" marriage relationship according to the plan of our Creator. Human sexuality refers to the spiritual, emotional, and physical pleasure derived from sexual intercourse which develops love, personality, unity, and permanence in husband-wife interpersonal relationships. This, in turn, furnishes an efficient home environment for growing, maturing children.

4. The fourth most important social influence is *education*—a thorough liberal arts education including the humanities, the natural sciences, and the social sciences. This need not be formal graduate level education that includes an M.A. and/or a Ph.D. degree. Education alone does not guarantee civilization. However, education that is honest, objective, and saturated with, and undergirded by, the religious and philosophical assumptions of Christianity is the servant of Christianity, the organized family, the organized community, and of civilization.

By nature I tend to be, and want to be, optimistic, because I feel that Christianity is basically optimistic. However, it is necessary to be realistic. For the past two decades I have been exceedingly concerned about the gradual erosion and decay of the morals, ethical standards, and values of the United States and the Western World. I have a conviction that the leading cause of this decay is the decline in the standards which should govern human sexuality. The forces that have triggered and promoted the decline in sexual morality have not come from within the organized churches or the family. Where have they originated? They have come from many sources such as vested interests, the mass media, social climbers, sinful human nature, and the indifference of the average citizen.

As a teacher of undergraduate Marriage and Family classes, my concern about the sexual moral decline led me to spend eleven years in study and research writing a book on *Sexual Happiness in Marriage** which was published in 1967. The purpose of the book was to help launch a counterattack against the moral decay of our society by rejecting the ascetic standards of the past and by uniting the forces of Christianity and sex as working partners—as they are united in the Scriptures. *Sexual Happiness in Marriage* is really a sex manual written for engaged couples and for married couples who may be somewhat unhappy in their sexual progress or may be floundering in their sexual experiences to the point that they are drifting fast toward separation and divorce. The book is written from a positive, Christian, and Biblical frame of reference, yet it gives details and techniques necessary for good sexual adjustment in marriage.

After the manuscript was finished, I became firmly convinced that I had covered only half of the area necessary to unite Christianity and human sexuality as cooperating friends in the normal processes of life. I had omitted the most important half, namely, sex education from puberty to marriage. I had written the last half first. Thus, when the *Sexual Happiness in Marriage* manuscript was finished, I began immediately on this second manuscript covering the general subject of "How to Understand and Control Sex from Puberty Until Marriage."

After I graduated from college, I spent three years studying in a theological seminary and followed this by twenty years as pastor of Baptist churches, where I emphasized a youth ministry. From the pastorate, I spent three years studying sociology in two universities, followed by twenty more years of teaching sociology in two undergraduate colleges, where I have specialized in teaching Marriage and Family courses. Thus my life experience has been in association with and service to youth. Therefore, the ideas and topics discussed in this volume come largely from four sources:

*Published by Zondervan Publishing House, Grand Rapids, Michigan.

1. Teaching college Marriage and Family classes for twenty years.
2. Student papers written on the topic of sex as related to the opinions, feelings, and problems of modern youth from puberty to marriage.
3. Small discussion groups on problems related to sex and courtship.
4. Dozens of personal counseling conferences with individual students or couples helping them with personal problems related to sex during courtship.

Thus, with a kind of 20-20 vision (twenty years in pastorates and twenty years in college classrooms), I send this book forth to be read by youth, their parents, their high school and college teachers and administrators, and the thousands of other youth leaders working in churches, youth camps and retreats, and in various other social agencies.

I hope this book will serve seven purposes:
1. Develop dialogue between youth and adults on the subject of sexual problems from puberty to marriage.
2. Help youth to understand their own sexual nature.
3. Help youth to decide what is sexually right and what is sexually wrong in courtship.
4. Develop efficient understanding between parents and their children on the subject of sex.
5. Help parents to be more positive, sympathetic, and understanding toward their children as they lead them through the years from puberty to marriage.
6. Help youth to develop a solid moral foundation and a mature mental, social, and Christian attitude toward sex in order that they may have an efficient and happy married life of personal fulfillment and self-realization.
7. Unite the forces of Christianity, the family, Christian youth, and education in a common counterattack against the rising forces of immorality in our society—to claim sex for Christianity.

Chapter One raises a series of questions that modern high school and college youth are asking about sex. Chapters Two through Twelve discuss the basic factors involved in these questions and attempt to give Christian answers. Appendix One is a formal discussion of the Biblical case for premarital chastity. Appendix Two gives a brief discussion of Judeo-Christian ontology as related to sex and morality. Appendix Three gives some suggestions to churches on sex education. Appendix Four presents a selected bibliography of current books written from a general Christian viewpoint on the subjects of sex education, courtship, marriage, and family life.

During the past five years I have become indebted to dozens of people who have made many contributions to the writing of this book, and this I gratefully acknowledge. I am deeply indebted to the following who have read parts or all of the manuscript and made many valuable suggestions: Charles C. Hobbs, college professor of English; David C. Cawood, physician and surgeon; Lewis E. Rhodes, clergyman; Millard J. Berquist, seminary president; Joe W. Burton, Editor of *Home Life* magazine; Henlee H. Barnette, seminary professor; Charles Earl, clergyman; William W. Stevens, college professor of Bible; and Chester A. Insko, seminary professor.

The writings and the Marriage and Family textbooks of Judson and Mary Landis, Paul Popenoe, Evelyn Millis Duvall, Henry A. Bowman, and David Mace have been a continual inspiration to me.

I am deeply indebted to five college students, Mrs. Marjorie Crowder Briggs, Dale Bunting, Ann Hunter, George Ellis and Carolyn Cole, who worked diligently with me as student advisors, for their frank, practical, and intelligent suggestions. I am grateful to three secretaries: Mrs. Judy Davidson and Mrs. Brenda Ellis, who typed the first draft, and Mrs. Amy Noland White, who typed the final manuscript.

CHAPTER 1

SOME HONEST QUESTIONS YOUTH ARE ASKING ABOUT SEX

So God created man in his own image, in the image of God he created him; male and female he created them ... And God saw everything that he had made, and behold, it was very good. (*Genesis 1:27, 31,* RSV)

For everything that God created is good, and nothing is to be rejected when it is taken with thanksgiving, since it is hallowed by God's own word and by prayer. *(I Timothy 4:4, 5,* NEB)

Robert, a tall, blond, senior science major, came to my office at ten o'clock on a warm spring day for a personal conference. The anxious expression on his face indicated that he was seriously concerned about something. When he attempted to explain the purpose of the conference, his eyes welled with tears; he turned his back and cried like a small child. I tried to give him support by explaining that tears are one of God's great blessings to us all and that there is no reason why we should be ashamed of them. When he turned around to talk to me, he was holding a diamond ring between two fingers.

He said, "Here is my problem. Ruth gave it back to me last night. It has been all my fault. I have mistreated her. If I could have one more chance, I would do right. Oh, if I could have just one more chance." Then he asked me if I would be willing to talk with her and try to persuade her to give him just one more chance.

"She knows you," he said. "She has been in your classes and has confidence in you," he pleaded.

We made an appointment for Ruth to come in for a conference at four o'clock that afternoon. When she came, she appeared relaxed and confident. She started the conversation by saying, "I am glad you are showing some interest in Robert. He needs your help." Later Ruth said, "I want it understood that my courtship relationship with Robert is ended. My decision is final, and I am going to be frank and tell you the real reason why I broke our engagement." At this point she was overcome with emotion. After a slight pause, and through sobs, she said slowly and firmly, "I am tired of drive-in theaters. I am tired of parking. I am tired of sex. I am tired of dating a man whose only interest seems to be sex. When I marry, I want to marry someone whose interest in me is something more than just sex." After hesitating again, she continued, "But please don't misunderstand me. I am not afraid of sex. In fact, I am looking forward to it in marriage. but I want to marry a man who is interested in me as a total person and who is interested in my total life. In this kind of marriage, sex will play its normal and beautiful role in our lives."

Later, I had two other conferences with Robert, attempting to help him pick up the pieces and plan a new life. I observed that he was a moral boy with lofty values and ideals. He had much personal potential. To have seduced his fiancee or any other woman was unthinkable to him. His attitude was that sex was a sacred something that belonged to marriage.

What had happened? Without realizing it, he had allowed his normal sex drive to be overemphasized in his courtship in the form of continuous "necking" and light "petting," to the point that he had destroyed what otherwise could have become a happily successful courtship. Across the years many other fine young people like Robert have fallen into this same kind of trap and have damaged or destroyed a potentially successful courtship and marriage.

There is a second type of attitude that tends to exalt sex as all-important but utterly impersonal. This is illustrated by Scott, another student. Outwardly he was an extremely personable young man. Yet with all his playboy-like charm, he was insecure, immature, and quite spoiled.

Scott first became aware of the opposite sex at the age of thirteen. This awareness came through a brief "look-see" experience with a girl his own age. At the age of sixteen, after a series of similar episodes, Scott experienced his first sexual intercourse with a girl he was dating. From this initial experience, Scott had one sexual conquest after another. A few months after he graduated from high school, he married a local girl with whom he had been engaging in sex on a regular basis. In six months their child was born, and shortly thereafter, they were divorced.

Their total relationship had been based upon a physical framework. When they took this framework away from their marriage, there was nothing left which could fill the void. Thus, the marriage collapsed, falling apart as if it were a straw house in a wind storm.

Today Scott is a student in a small state college. He seems to have learned nothing from his past experiences. On dates if a girl does not yield immediately to his sexual wishes, he maneuvers and persuades her until her resistance is broken down, and she ultimately gives in to his demands. He sees a girl as nothing but a sexual opportunity. In his thinking, waiting for sex until marriage went out with the Model T Ford. He wants what he wants when he wants it. To Scott, sex has become a pleasurable plaything, a toy. He willfully forces and exploits other persons. He is devoid of feelings such as kindness, tenderness, and love. He is totally blind to the fact that this is not the kind of foundation upon which a completely satisfactory marriage relationship can be built.

These two young men, Robert and Scott, are symbolic of many youth who are confused about sex. One might well ask whether Robert would have experienced his heartbreaking situation had he controlled his sex drive and directed it by Christian principles. One might also ask whether Scott would be the kind of person he is today had he been shown the Christian view of sex and its relationship to marriage. Dogmatic answers to these boys' problems cannot be given; what is certain, however, is that unless someone gives honest answers to the questions being asked by you, the reader, as today's young people, a tidal wave of sexual permissiveness may well sweep over you and leave terrible devastation in its wake.

Let us consider the questions you are asking today about sex. I asked two Marriage and Family classes composed of college sophomores, juniors and seniors to write a short paper listing ten pertinent questions that they had heard modern high school and college youth ask about sex. The following list is a summary of the questions asked most frequently.

1. Why have my attitudes and feelings about the opposite sex changed since I was a child?
2. Why is there a communication gap between children and their parents on the subject of sex? Is the gap narrowing or growing wider? How can we bridge this gap?
3. Are other young people concerned about sex, and do they think about it as I do?
4. What is the difference between "like" and "love"?
5. Can true love emotions be separated from sexual attraction during courtship?
6. Is it all right to kiss a boy or girl on the first date? How many dates should I have before the first kiss? What should a kiss mean? Does a couple have to be in love before they kiss?
7. Can a couple practice prolonged kissing without taking further steps that lead to sexual intercourse?

8. Should there be petting on the first several casual dates when a couple is not in love? Why should I not pet and make out when all the others in my group do? What will be the consequences to me if I do not?
9. What do I want and need in a husband or wife?
10. Why is premarital sexual intercourse wrong?
11. If premarital sexual relations are wrong, why do we have such a strong desire for them?
12. Doesn't the "New Morality" make our past sexual traditions out of date? Isn't the "New Morality" positive while our traditional sex attitudes are negative?
13. Aren't sex relations with my boyfriend or girlfriend my own business? Is it really any of society's business? If so, why?
14. Are the morals that have been taught to me by my parents right for me today?
15. Does a person really have to live by rules and regulations? Why can't we be free? Hasn't scientific fact set aside all moral rules and regulations as superstition?
16. If we have to live by rules, does the individual person, the couple involved, society, or God set up the rules that determine what is right and what is wrong? Can rules be made that are satisfactory to all four?
17. Why does society have such a double standard? How can we get rid of it?
18. Why don't the churches provide more positive help for youth in the area of sex? If "Hollywood sex" is to be so highly advertised, why shouldn't the benefits of married sex life be made known to youth? Why don't the churches and society take more definite steps to control "mass media" sex advertisements? Aren't the churches partly responsible for the warped and twisted view youth receives when they turn to pulp magazines?

19. Why do some parents and church people tell youth that sex outside of marriage is wrong, and then engage in extramarital affairs, or act as if an affair would really be exciting?

20. Where and when should a couple draw the line between right and wrong? How far can a couple go without sacrificing their spiritual and moral values and at the same time enjoy a rewarding love expression with each other?

21. Who should draw the line on how far a couple should go in petting—the boy, the girl, or both? Why do so many people say that it is the girl's responsibility to control petting situations? Does the boy's quick sexual arousal throw the responsibility to control petting situations entirely upon the girl? Shouldn't it be equal?

22. Is it right for society to blame the boy because the Creator gave him a strong sex drive?

23. Do boys or girls really care whether they marry a virgin or not? Why is it that boys want to marry a virgin, yet overlook their own promiscuity? Is the desire to marry a virgin a legitimate concern in marriage plans?

24. Assuming true love is justification for limited premarital love expression, what should be the pattern of affection during the going steady and engagement periods insofar as bodily contact is concerned? Is petting really necessary during courtship?

25. Is sexual intercourse permissible between engaged couples? Often couples say, "We have found each other; we love each other; we are engaged; we plan to be married soon; why should we wait any longer to give ourselves completely to each other?" What is the difference between an engaged couple three weeks or three months before marriage and the same couple three weeks or three months after marriage?

26. How do I know what kind of sex partner I will make without premarital sexual experience? How do I know that my future spouse will be sexually compatible in marriage without premarital experience? Will we really know even if we do have some premarital sexual experience?
27. Isn't guilt feeling about premarital sex an invention of primitive and underdeveloped cultures and religions that has been handed down to our civilized, scientific cultures?
28. Should a couple feel guilty if they by accident go all the way? What should a couple do if they go all the way, but do so only once?
29. How should we control the situation which leads to petting problems?
30. Should a boy/girl confess previous sexual experiences to his/her fiance?
31. How can a person be forgiven for past sexual sins? Will God forgive a boy/girl if he/she goes all the way and then never marries?
32. Should birth control pills be made available to unmarried girls to reduce premarital pregnancy?
33. Is the control of sexual desire during courtship harmful to later sexual happiness in marriage?
34. Is it wrong to have thoughts about sex relations with the boy or girl you love, are engaged to, and plan to marry?
35. What basic spiritual, moral, and social values should youth look for in today's world?

These are only a few of the many and varied questions asked today. They are sensible, honest, intelligent, and practical questions that are pertinent to your future years. These are inquiries into a subject that not one single teen-ager is able to escape. The questions deserve sensible, honest, intelligent, and practical answers. They deserve Christian answers. Surely, the questions are frank, and to the point and may cause some parents to squirm in embarrassment. True, the resulting answers may pack a tremendous punch, but it would be far more devastating if these questions were never raised, and even more damaging if honest replies were never given. It must be realized that the world is for the young—as it always has been—to taste, to smell, to feel, to hear, to understand, and to experience.

There is a central theme prevalent in the above questions that seems to characterize the behavior of the "in-group" of today's youth. This idea is that these questions concerning sex and the various other social changes have just been invented by this generation. Actually, what has really happened is that old things merely take on a slightly new garment in each new generation. We must acknowledge that beards have come and gone throughout history, that a guitar is simply a grown-up ukulele, and, by the way, that boys in bell-bottom trousers and raccoon coats were in "style" a generation ago. When I worked in a shoe factory many years ago, long sideburns were popular with the "in-group." When I was a boy, I wanted a Model T just as much as many of you want a Jaguar. And some of the songs of my day were slightly beneath classical music, for example, "Itty Bitty Fishy Inna Itta Poo" and "Mares E Dotes and Does E Dotes, and Little Lambs E Divy." Really, is there much difference? The truth is that the youth of my generation asked, or wanted to ask, all of these questions. If they did not ask them, it was because they knew no one in those days would dare offer an honest answer. Today only the social and cultural framework has changed. And the Christian community must not go on, generation after generation, blundering, groping, and neglecting pertinent sex education of youth.

In the past, many adults have habitually referred to the teen years in language that tends to ridicule or condemn young people. This is unfortunate. It goes against the grain of the growing, unfolding, insecure youth who needs so badly to be loved and understood. When I was in my early teens, adult neighbors and friends would "kid" me about being at that "awkward" age. They said I was climbing "fool's hill." Those good people meant well, but their language was cruel. Being a rather quiet boy, I did not attempt to defend myself, but inside, I seethed with anger. I felt misunderstood, mistreated, and neglected. Today, many well-meaning adults say, "He is just an inexperienced teen-ager." "Maybe someday he will grow up. . . ." They use different words than those addressed to me, but the results are the same.

When you reach puberty, you already have considerable knowledge and capacity. At the same time, you have many limitations and are dependent upon your parents and society for many things. And yet, one day you will be our authors, college presidents, clergymen, jet pilots, surgeons, major league stars, and U. S. senators. Your future is bright and certain; therefore, your teen years ought to be happy, confident years of increasing knowledge and personality progress.

Most Christian young people want to do what is right; you want to follow God's plan for your lives. You want to be Christians—mature Christians. You want a stable, permanent marriage. You want to live a full, complete, creative life—to be good citizens and good friends to other people. Yet, because you are human, you are tempted both to reject Christian moral standards and to be swept along with the strong cultural current of sexual freedom. You must have help and trusted guidance.

Some of you may outwardly act rebellious to cover your lack of knowledge and, therefore, your insecurity. But inside, you really long for the Christian adult world to tell you in clear and precise language what is right and what is wrong in the area of sex. Christian adults must answer your questions.

Notice what a military field commander does when his front line positions are overrun by the enemy. He orders a major counterattack. And so must we! You as youth need to know how sex fits into the total picture of courtship, marriage, the family and community life.

Some Honest Questions Youth Are Asking About Sex

The pages that follow are an "all-out" counterattack against the advancing immoral forces of our day. It is my hope that the Roberts and the Scotts and thousands of other young people will be inspired to a solid Christian faith that will help them to reject and overcome the evil and tempting situations in which they find themselves. It is my prayer that these truths about sex will serve as a launching pad to help those of you in the teens and early twenties to think through the whole area of personal sexual control intelligently.

CHAPTER 2

UNDERSTANDING YOUR PARENTS AND
YOUR PRESENT IDEAS ABOUT SEX

When I was a little child I talked and felt and thought like a little child. Now that I am a man my childish speech and feeling and thought have no further significance for me.

At present we are men looking at puzzling reflections in a mirror. The time will come when we shall see reality whole and face to face! At present all I know is a little fraction of the truth, but the time will come when I shall know it as fully as God now knows me! (*I Corinthians 13:11, 12*, Phillips)

The realistic viewpoint is to recognize that the alternatives are not whether children should or should not know about sex. The only choice that parents have is between the child's getting garbled information from random sources or receiving at least a part of his sex information from the parents who are interested in his healthy emotional development.

(Judson and Mary Landis, *Building a Successful Marriage*)

To control sex properly until marriage, it is important for you to understand your present attitudes and ideas about sex. It is especially important that you understand the *sources* of your knowledge about sex; that is, the personal, family, and social circumstances that brought about this knowledge. How did you acquire your present ideas about sex? From parents? From brothers and sisters? From grandparents? From other relatives? From friends? From self-exploration? From observing animals? From books? If you are like most teen-agers, your information probably came from a cross-section of all these sources.

Ask yourself this question: From which source would you really rather have had this information? Be honest with yourself. Wouldn't mom and dad have been your first choice, especially if they could have informed you honestly, simply, and in a manner that was not embarrassing? Regardless of your answer, I am sure you remember vividly those confusing, weird, misleading, and distasteful remarks heard about sex outside your home. Wouldn't it have been much better if you could have heard this information from a reputable source? Well, this is one of the big aims of this book — to be a valuable and reliable source of information for answers to youth's questions about sex and to help them reject those false ideas and absurdities which have led many of them into frustration, doubt, and confusion in the past.

Listen to Diane, a lovely girl who is twenty-one and engaged, tell about her situation which may be similar to the experience of many.

"To this day," related Diane bitterly, "my mother has never taken the time to talk to me about sex in any form. When I was a child," she continued, "mom often avoided my questions altogether. The only time she told me anything was when my menstrual cycle began, and that was only on how to keep myself clean and dainty. I was told never to say anything about it to boys. When I asked her how a baby started growing in her stomach, mom replied: 'The stork left it there and the doctor will take it out when the time comes.' When I inquired a second time about how the baby got there, mom said: 'You have plenty of time to learn about this later on in life. Don't worry about it now.' But that time never arrived. My knowledge came from books and from my friends. To tell you the truth, I have been cheated by my own parents." Then Diane added sadly, "I feel very resentful about it all."

Boys, also, often have the same experience. Ted, in relating his personal experience of sex education in his home, remarked, "If I were to write on paper what my parents taught me, I would be finished before I began. I never heard a word about sex spoken in my home. My parents, though, did express disapproval of some of my friends, suggestive movies, or of improper language by stating that these were 'not nice.' Instead of recognizing that the physical change that was occurring in me was a normal part of growing up, I got the feeling it must be something bad. When I heard my friends talk, or when I read about sex in books, I was disgusted and considered it ridiculous, distasteful, and vulgar. It was only through my church background, and through friends' opinions that were contrary to mine, that I began to see sex in a different light. In fact," Ted stated emphatically, "I accepted sex outwardly much sooner than I did inwardly. I now feel that if I had received my sex education firsthand from my parents, I would not have had to travel the long, hard road of frustration that I did."

But we must not think that all parents are failures at teaching their children about sex. Our research, done among 426 college students, sophomores, juniors, and seniors, indicated that 55 per cent of parents did excellent or fair in giving their children sex education, while the parents of 45 per cent of the students did poorly or gave their children little or no sex education. Actually, parents and society are doing a better job of sex education now than they did ten or twenty years ago.

Some parents have swallowed their embarrassment and have talked with their children about sex in an organized and constructive manner. Gail was one of the fortunate ones whose parents exercised the positive approach to sex. This is the way she tells her story: "My parents have always been available when I needed them; they were broad-minded, frank, and explained things to me at my own age level. I was never embarrassed to ask either of them questions. Even though I was a girl, dad let it be known that I could talk to him as well as to mother.

"I cannot remember when my parents did not talk to me frankly about sex. During the summer when I was ten years old, my mother gave me a book entitled *What Girls Should Know About Sex*. I read one chapter each day, and when I had finished she would discuss the chapter with me by asking me questions and by having me ask her questions. I looked forward to these talks each evening. Often we would chat for an hour or longer on each chapter. As I look back upon these frank talks, they stand out as some of the sweetest, most beautiful, and most meaningful experiences of my life. From that summer until now, my parents and I have been very close. I would not trade this relationship with my parents for anything in the world."

We all rejoice with Gail and other young people whose parents did a good job in their sex education. However, I would like to speak a word in defense of the parents of Diane and Ted and the many thousands of young people who feel their parents failed them in sex education. This defense is an honest effort to help both teens and their parents to understand themselves a little better. Often teen-agers expect their parents to be perfect in everything. This is expecting too much. Most parents are not doctors, sociologists, or psychologists. In fact, we may be rather certain that most parents who rated poorly in the area of sex education had parents who taught them *nothing* on sex, and many of them never had a course in biology, health, or sociology in their lives. Parents are really a product of their own childhood and the way they were reared by their families. Since sex and the idea of sex education was not openly discussed in their youth, it is quite natural that it would be difficult for them to make this transition today. It is not easy for them to let go of the old stigmas attached to sex which were ingrained in them during childhood. Consequently, it causes parents embarrassment and insecurity when their own children approach them on this subject.

Furthermore, it is not a willful or spiteful decision of parents not to talk to their children about sex. Actually, most parents really want to instruct their children, but in their insecurity, lack of experience, and false embarrassment, words fail them. Many fine parents have spent agonizing hours over this problem.

One day after I had discussed parents' responsibilities in a college Marriage and Family class, Russell, a married senior, stopped by after class to relate his experience.

He said, "My father is a well-known, successful medical doctor and surgeon. He did not say one word to me about sex all of my life until three days before my wedding. As my wedding date approached, I could tell that the matter was weighing on my father's mind. Finally, he called me in to talk with him. His face was white, and his hands were literally trembling. In a quivering voice he talked briefly about sex in marriage. For his sake, I was glad when he finished. The things he said in the brief conversation were simple ideas that I had known for years." Russell continued by saying, "My father is a good man. He is moral. He does not smoke or drink alcohol; he is honest, and by his example he has taught me many solid social values. I have been fortunate in having such a wonderful father. Therefore, I am not bitter toward him for his neglect in the area of sex."

If you were fortunate enough to have parents who dealt with you wisely about sex, you should be exceedingly thankful to God all the days of your life. However, those whose parents failed them in sex education should not become bitter toward their parents. Instead, attempt to understand your parents and always be open for a good future parent-child relationship. Secondly, make every possible effort to understand your own present attitudes and ideas about sex, where you got them, and why.

For example, insecure teen-age boys often boast about their sexual achievements and exploits, experiences that probably never really happened. This false bragging is a futile effort to bolster inner fears and insecurity. But it may cause innocent listeners to feel that there is something wrong with themselves. They may begin to form wrong ideas about themselves, such as "I must not be normal," or "I must be inadequate sexually." Such ideas tend to take root and grow. Or, a girl may have had the harrowing experience of rape or an attempted rape, and this experience may cause her to think that sex is sinful and that all men are evil. Many incidents, some important and some not so important, may cause a growing child to fear sex or to think of it as evil.

Doris, who was unhappy with her early married sex life, came to me for help. In beginning the conference that day she said, "When I was a child, I developed some false ideas about sex, and I want to talk to a marriage counselor to help shake me loose from these ideas so that I can have a happier marriage." Later in the conversation, she told of an experience she had had as a seven-year-old girl. She was sleeping in the same room with her parents. Through the weeks she had suspected them of doing things she did not understand. So one night she feigned sleep. Her parents, planning sex relations in their bed nearby, wanted to be sure she was asleep. Her mother said in a rather loud voice, "Doris, are you asleep?" Doris did not answer or move and continued to pretend to be asleep. Then she heard her mother say, "She is asleep; we can go ahead." Doris listened and heard, but did not understand.

The next day she was afraid to talk to her mother. The experience caused her to feel she was rejected by her parents. They had some secret which for some reason they refused to share with her. She wondered why her parents would keep a secret from her. "They must not love me; there must be something wrong with me," she told herself. In the days ahead, she tried hard to please her parents so that they would love her. The harder she tried, the more frustrated she became. A few years later when Doris learned enough at school to know what her parents were doing, it caused her to hate sex. This feeling continued to grow and now it was causing her difficulty in her married life.

There is no easy approach that parents can take in teaching their children about the mysteries of their own bodies. It is not as simple as black and white, as youth sometimes seem to assume. Sexual understanding is not something that parents can impart when a certain day arrives. It is a *continuous process over a span of years from a child's first inquiry until the day he marries*. It may be likened to a bud on a tree which first comes forth as a small nodule on the twig. With time and the right amount of sunshine and rain necessary for growth, the bud bursts forth as a full, beautiful, mature bloom. God's creation! His handiwork! So it is with children who are also creatures of God's handiwork, created in His image. If they do not receive the right and wholesome knowledge for growth, they will surely not develop into the graceful, happy, healthy, mature persons God intended them to become.

CHAPTER 3

REPRODUCTIVE AND SEXUAL ORGANS

Have you not read that he who made them from the beginning made them male and female? *(Matthew 19:4,* RSV)

Now the body is not one member but many. . . . God has harmonised the whole body by giving importance of function to the parts . . . that the body should work together as a whole with all the members in sympathetic relationship with one another. *(I Corinthians 12:14, 24, 25,* Phillips)

It is not only important that you understand the Christian point of view on sexuality, but it is also necessary that you understand the nature and purpose of the human reproductive and sexual organs.

This chapter will present a brief sketch of both the male and female reproductive and sexual organs.[1] The discussion should be understood in light of the Christian doctrine of sexuality. If this part of human life is rightly understood, it should increase our faith in God. There are many sources of evidence pointing to the existence of God. One of the more important of these evidences is the wonderful, intricate, complex structure of the human body. This is equally true of the reproductive and sexual systems, each of which is part of the total unit, the body. Again and again, as we study the plan and

[1] Chapter Three is a revision of Chapter Three from *Sexual Happiness in Marriage,* Zondervan, 1967. Used by permission.

purpose of these systems, there is abundant evidence of purposive planning by God, our Creator.

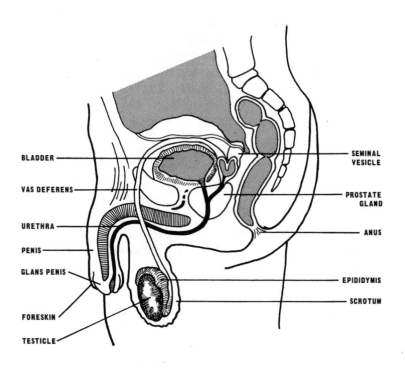

BLADDER

VAS DEFERENS

URETHRA

PENIS

GLANS PENIS

FORESKIN

TESTICLE

SEMINAL VESICLE

PROSTATE GLAND

ANUS

EPIDIDYMIS

SCROTUM

FIGURE ONE. MALE REPRODUCTIVE AND SEXUAL ORGANS

GONADS (gō′nads). The two gonads, sometimes called *sex glands, testes (tes′tēz),* or *testicles (tes′ti kəls),* are oval-shaped organs and may be called the "factory" which reproduces *spermatozoa (spûr′mə təzō′ə).* Spermatozoa means "living thing." Usually, in popular language, the spermatozoa are called "sperm" cells. These are the male reproductive cells that unite with the female reproductive cells in order for human life to be reproduced. Also, the gonads produce a male sex hormone called *testosterone (te stos'tə rōn')* which plays a vital part in producing male body characteristics such as body shape, voice, hair, etc. The process of reproducing sperm cells begins at approximately age thirteen to fourteen. This period in a boy's life is called puberty. The production of these cells continues in healthy males past middle age, and often on into old age. The gonads are enclosed in the *scrotum (skrō'təm)* which is a fleshy sac suspended between the thighs and united to the body torso.

EPIDYMIS *(ep'i did'ə mis)*. The Greek "epi" means "upon" and "didymis" means "gonad." Thus; the epididymis is that which is upon the gonad. It is a coiled tube attached to the top of the gonad. The sperm cells move out of the gonad into the epididymis where they remain for a time, while they mature. The epididymis is often called a temporary storage vessel for the sperm cells.

VAS DEFERENS *(vas def'ə renz')*. The Latin "vas" means "vessel" and "deferens" means "to carry." Thus, the vas deferens is a "vessel for carrying something." It is a long tube connected with the epididymis. It moves out of the scrotum into the body cavity through a small opening of muscles in the abdominal wall. Inside the body cavity, the vas deferens eventually empties into the *urethra (yōō rē'thrə)*, the tube inside the penis that also drains the bladder.

SEMINAL VESICLE *(sem'ə nəl ves'i kəl)*. The word "seminal" means "semen." *Semen (sē'mən)* is made up of sperm cells and a fluid that carries the sperm. The word "vesicle" means "vessel" or "sac." Although the seminal vesicle appears to serve as a second temporary storage reservoir, it shares this responsibility with the *ampulla (am pul'ə)*. The ampulla is the enlarged upper end of the vas deferens. The seminal vesicle also secretes a fluid which becomes a part of the semen.

PROSTATE GLAND *(pros'tāt)*. The prostate gland is muscular and glandular. It produces a secretion that becomes a part of the semen. The muscular part of the prostate gland together with the seminal vesicle and the rigid penis contract and ejaculate (discharge) the semen through the urethra and to the outside of the body.

PENIS *(pē'nis)*. The penis is both an internal and an external organ. It is composed of porous tissues which are a honeycombed network of blood vessels. Under sexual stimulation, blood rushes into these blood vessels. At the same time, small valves are automatically closed, preventing the blood from flowing out. As stimulation continues, blood flows in, the penis fills up, tightens, and stands rigid and erect. When stimulation ceases, or an ejaculation takes place, the small valves gradually open and the excess blood flows back into the blood system. This process of the ejaculation of the semen is called *orgasm (ôr'gaz əm)*, popularly called a "climax." This system of erection of the penis and ejaculation of the semen, for the purpose of depositing it in the vagina of the female to bring about conception, is a major and skillful engineering accomplishment on the part of the divine Creator.

When the penis is in the relaxed state, it is about 3-1/2 to 4 inches in length. In its state of erection, it is about 5 to 6-1/2 inches in length.

The head of the penis is called *glans penis* and is a little larger than the shaft of the penis. The glans penis contains a heavy concentration of nerve endings which play a major role in the sexual arousal of the male. These nerve endings are no different than those in other parts of the body except they are more densely concentrated in the glans penis. Usually, at birth, the glans penis is encircled with a thick layer of skin called *prepuce (prē'pyoos)* or *foreskin*. It is important that the opening in the foreskin of the adult male be large enough to

Reproductive and Sexual Organs

allow movement back and forth over the head of the erect penis without pain or excess tightness. When this condition does not prevail, the person needs to be circumcised. Circumcision is a simple operation in which a surgeon cuts the top of the foreskin away, thus freeing the glans penis from its covering. The purpose of circumcision is twofold: (1) to permit effective sanitation and (2) to permit normal sexual experiences and sexual control. Although the Jews used circumcision as a religious symbol, there is evidence that they possessed insight concerning its practicality. (At the birth of a male child, couples should instruct the attending physician to perform circumcision, if it is needed.) Circumcision of the male is also thought to help in preventing cancer of the cervix in the female.

SEMINAL OR NOCTURNAL EMISSIONS. Under sexual stimulation, when the epididymis, the external storage tank for sperm cells, is full, the sperm cells are moved out of the epididymis through the vas deferens into the body cavity to be lodged in the internal storage tank, the seminal vesicle. When both the external and internal storage tanks are filled with semen, the sexual interest and drive of the person comes alive and is ripe for release. Under these circumstances the person is easily aroused sexually. For married men this sexual drive is released through normal sexual intercourse with their wives. For single men the Creator has provided an automatic sexual release usually called "seminal emissions" or "nocturnal emissions." "Emission" means "to send out" or "to throw out" and "nocturnal" means "night." When the semen reservoirs are filled, during sleep there is an automatic sexual ejaculation or emission of the semen by way of the urethra. What actually happens is that during the night's six to eight hours' sleep the male bladder fills with urine. This swelling of the bladder presses against the seminal vesicle which is full of semen, and the pressure amounts to automatic sexual stimulation during sleep. Thus the penis becomes erect, and the automatic sexual stimulation triggers an orgasm during sleep. During these nocturnal emissions the person involved may or may not awaken. The automatic nocturnal orgasms are natural and normal during the teen and youth years until marriage. A young man should not think of them as being nasty or sinful, and he should not have guilt feelings about them. They are simply a part of the total sexual organization of man planned by our wonderful Creator. God created man with his strong sex drive and purposely gave him this automatic release to help him control it until he is mature enough for marriage. The fact that these nocturnal emissions slightly spot or soil the bed linens is a minor matter that is understood by a boy's mother, who launders the bed linens.

There is a small percentage of young men, less than five percent, who never have these nightly emissions. This does not mean that they are in any way abnormal sexually. They can look forward to a normal sex life in marriage.

It is recommended that young men lean on these seminal emissions as a means of sexual control until marriage. The very fact of the existence of nocturnal seminal emissions is strong evidence that the Creator did not mean for single young men to have sexual intercourse until marriage. This problem of sexual intercourse before marriage will be discussed in detail in Chapters 4, 7, 8 and Appendix I. The possibility of a boy using masturbation as a means of sexual self-control will be discussed in Chapter 9.

FEMALE REPRODUCTIVE AND SEXUAL ORGANS

LABIA MAJORA *(lā'bē ə majōr'ə)*. The Latin "labia" means "lips" and "majora" means "major or large." The labia majora are large lips, composed of thick, round, fleshy folds of tissue, covered with hair. They protect the genital organs beneath, which are covered with tender mucous membrane.

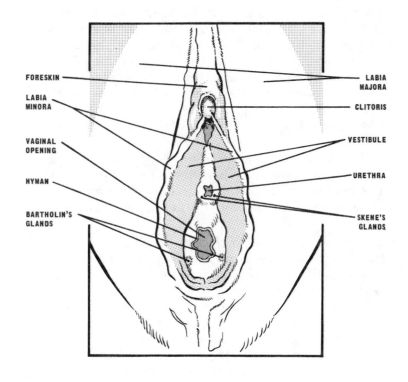

FORESKIN

LABIA
MINORA

VAGINAL
OPENING

HYMAN

BARTHOLIN'S
GLANDS

LABIA
MAJORA

CLITORIS

VESTIBULE

URETHRA

SKENE'S
GLANDS

FIGURE THREE. VULVA OR EXTERNAL FEMALE ORGANS

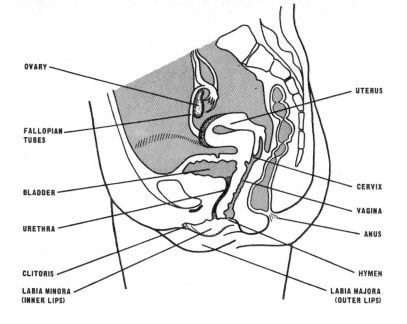

FIGURE TWO. FEMALE REPRODUCTIVE AND SEXUAL ORGANS

Labels on figure:
- OVARY
- UTERUS
- FALLOPIAN TUBES
- BLADDER
- CERVIX
- VAGINA
- URETHRA
- ANUS
- CLITORIS
- HYMEN
- LABIA MINORA (INNER LIPS)
- LABIA MAJORA (OUTER LIPS)

LABIA MINORA *(lā'bē ə mi nōr'ə)*. The Latin "labia minora" means "small lips." They are located inside the large outer lips. They are small thin folds of tissue covered with mucous membrane.

CLITORIS *(klit'ər is)*. The word "clitoris" is derived from the Greek word *kleitoris* meaning "to shut up." This has reference to the organ being concealed by the outer and inner lips. The clitoris in the female corresponds with the penis in the male. It is located at the outer uppermost point where the inner lips meet. It is similar to the penis in two ways. (1) It is composed of a shaft, glans (head), and prepuce (foreskin). The foreskin is a small hood that partially covers the clitoris. It is made up of the inner lips at the point where they join together. (2) The glans of the clitoris is composed of a dense concentration of nerve endings, designed to produce sexual arousal when under stimulation. The clitoris is different from the penis in that (1) it has no opening, (2) it ejaculates nothing, and (3) it does not directly play a part in the process of reproduction. It is exclusively

Reproductive and Sexual Organs

41

an organ of sexual sensation. It is the external trigger that sets off sexual arousal and orgasm.

The labia majora, labia minora, and the clitoris make up the external female organs. They are often called the *vulva* or *genitals.*

VAGINA *(və jī'nə).* The word "vagina" is a Latin word meaning "scabbard," that is, a sheath that encloses a sword or bayonet, to shield and protect it. The vagina is the passage between the vulva and the womb that receives the male penis in sexual intercourse. It is composed of elastic, mucous membrane which lays in wrinkles. Normally it is approximately three and one-half inches in length, but it can stretch to six or more inches in length without discomfort. It is also a reproductive organ, in that it is the passageway for the menstrual flow and is the birth canal.

HYMEN *(hī'mən).* The word "hymen" is a Greek word meaning "skin" or "membrane." The hymen is a fold of mucous membrane partly enclosing the opening of the vagina. It generally tends to block sexual intercourse. It varies in size, structure, and thickness. In a few (very few) cases the hymen is entirely absent. In some cases the hymen may possibly be broken by some excessive physical activity or by a physical accident. In other cases, it may be necessary for a physician to break the hymen for medical purposes. On the other hand some hymens are so thick and strong that it is impossible to break them in sexual intercourse. When this is the case, it is necessary to have a physician stretch or cut the membrane. This may be determined at the time of the pre-marital pelvic examination. When a hymen is broken in first intercourse, there may be slight or considerable pain and some bleeding. The amount of pain and bleeding would be determined by the structure and thickness of the hymen.

UTERUS *(yōō'tər əs).* The word "uterus" is a Latin word usually translated "womb." The uterus or womb *(wōōm)* is a pear-shaped muscular organ about three and one-half inches long and two and one-half inches wide. It is the home in which the human embryo is protected and developed before birth. The smaller end of the uterus opens into the upper portion of the vagina and is known as the *cervix (sûr'viks)*. The opening between the uterus and the vagina is called the mouth of the cervix. The muscular strength of the walls of the uterus is the major force which expels the baby through the vaginal passage at birth.

OVARY *(ō'və rē)*. The word "ovary" is a form of the Latin word "ovum" which means "egg." The female ovaries correspond to the male gonads. Besides producing hormones, which determine the female body characteristics, the ovaries produce reproductive cells called "ova." In popular language the ova ("ovum" is singular) are usually called "egg" cells.

FALLOPIAN TUBES *(fə lō'pē ən)*. The word "Fallopian" is the name of an Italian anatomist who did much research related to the Fallopian tubes. These two tubes are the passageways from the ovaries to the uterus. Each tube is about four inches in length. They are not directly connected to the ovaries. The finger-like projections of the larger end of the tubes intercept the egg cell when it is released from the ovary and start it on its way to the uterus.

CONCEPTION. Young couples, ready for marriage, need to understand the basic processes involved in the nature of conception and of menstruation. One egg is released from an ovary each month or on the average of every twenty-eight days. The release of the egg from the ovary is called the *ovulation* period.

There are approximately 1,000,000 sperm cells in each male ejaculation (orgasm). When sperm cells are deposited in the vagina, they travel quickly through the cervical opening into the uterus and scatter throughout the Fallopian tubes. For conception to occur, sexual intercourse must take place at, or near, the time of the ovulation period. Medical science is not certain about

Reproductive and Sexual Organs

43

the life span of the egg and the sperm. Some scholars suggest about twelve hours for the egg and twenty-four hours for the sperm. Others suggest forty-eight to seventy-two hours for both egg and sperm. When a live egg cell encounters a live sperm cell, the two unite and conception is accomplished. Usually, conception occurs in the Fallopian tubes. The fertilized egg is moved gradually, over a period of three to five days, through the Fallopian tubes into the uterus. Here it is implanted on the wall of the uterus and gradually develops for a period of approximately nine months. The period from conception to birth is called pregnancy.

The *menstrual* period is a vital part of the reproductive nature of women. The word "menstrual" is derived from a Latin word "mensis" meaning "month." During the period in which the egg cell is being developed in the ovary, the lining inside the uterus increases in thickness and an extra supply of blood comes into it. The increased lining of the uterus is for the purpose of anchoring the fertilized egg, and the extra supply of blood is for nourishing it during its development. When no sperm cell is present to fertilize the egg, it soon dies, and the preparations that have been taking place inside the uterus are now useless. Therefore the increased lining of the uterus and the increased supply of blood are expelled from the body through the vagina, and the process starts over again. This monthly cycle begins at approximately age twelve to thirteen (puberty) and continues until approximately age forty-five to fifty. The ceasing of this cycle is called *menopause*. The word "menopause" comes from two Greek words and means "to cease" or "to stop."

The process of reproduction and the process of the menstrual cycle are two more examples of major engineering achievements planned by the infinite mind of the Creator-God.

THE SO-CALLED SAFE PERIOD. Judson and Mary Landis state that after sexual intercourse, if a sperm cell encounters an egg cell, "the sperm cell unites with the egg cell and conception has occurred."[2] This is a simple yet a profound statement, dealing with what is essentially a Divine miracle. Only under these circumstances can human reproduction take place.

One might ask at what period during the menstrual cycle can a girl become pregnant. A girl can become pregnant only when the egg cell has been sent out of the ovary and becomes located in the Fallopian tubes or the womb. Our problem is that we do not know exactly when the egg cell will be expelled from the ovary. Usually the egg is expelled during the middle of the twenty-eight-day menstrual cycle. Assuming a regular twenty-eight-day menstrual cycle, the ovulation period should take place at the end of the fourteenth day or between the fourteenth and fifteenth days. To arrive at this day, begin at the first day of the menstrual cycle and count fourteen days.

The theory of the so-called "safe" period assumes that if a married couple avoids having sexual intercourse two or three days on each side of the ovulation period, there will be no danger of a wife becoming pregnant during the rest of the days of the menstrual cycle. In general terms there is truth to this assumption. However, there are so many other complex factors involved that the so-called "safe" period may not be safe at all. Women are not machines that operate on a mechanical basis. They are individual persons living in a world of ideas, possessing emotions, feelings, sentiments, and values, all of which affect bodily functions — including menstrual cycle and ovulation period. The cycle may also be affected by physical health problems, and mental and emotional stress and strain.

A few women release more than one egg at different times during a single menstrual cycle. Medical science

[2] Judson T. and Mary G. Landis, *Building a Successful Marriage,* Prentice-Hall, Inc., 1968, 5th Edition, p. 415. Used by permission.

Reproductive and Sexual Organs

45

has verified a pregnancy taking place at every day during the total cycle. Thus, there is really no dependable "safe" period.

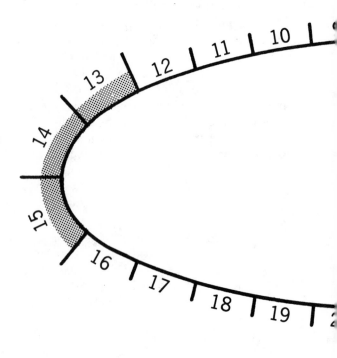

OVULATION PERIOD
MENSTRUAL PERIOD

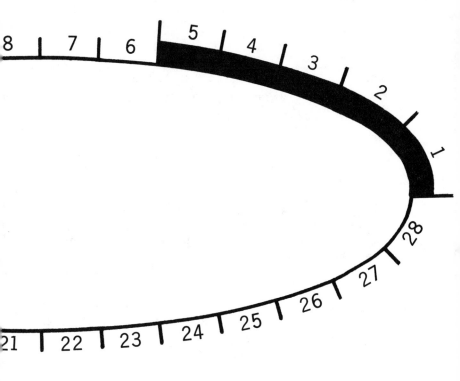

Figure Four. The Menstrual Cycle and So-Called Safe Period

CHAPTER 4

WHY SOCIETY OBJECTS TO PREMARITAL SEX RELATIONS

Righteousness exalts a nation, but sin is a reproach to any people. *(Proverbs 14:34,* RSV)

Society and its members are part of an indivisible whole. Only a sick individual ignores his society and his responsibilities to it. On the other hand, a healthy society cannot ignore the welfare of its members but must take an interest in their lives, even though the attention is not always welcome.

(John W. Drakeford, *The Great Sex Swindle)*

The questions most often asked by youth about sex are: "Why is sexual intercourse wrong before marriage? Why do my parents, my church, and my community object? Will you please tell me in clear and precise language the reasons why it is wrong?"

The answers to these questions are complex but can be stated in simple language. Let me outline nine major reasons why society objects to premarital intercourse.

1. Probably society's first and greatest objection to premarital sexual intercourse is *the ever present danger of a premarital pregnancy.* It is true that modern scientific achievements have made and will continue to make great strides in controlling parenthood. However, most teen-agers do not have access to effective contraceptives (devices used to prevent pregnancy). They have neither sufficient and reliable knowledge about the nature of

sex and reproduction, nor the experience and the maturity necessary to control birth. Therefore, in spite of modern planned parenthood knowledge, premarital pregnancies have been increasing for the past fifty years. The national social welfare agencies indicate that annually there are as many as 350,000 recorded premarital pregnancies in the United States. This 350,000 does not include the multitudes of unrecorded cases or the cases of abortion and forced miscarriage.

When there is a premarital pregnancy, the social and personal damage that follows through the coming months, years, and throughout life can be tragic. The damage is greatest to the girl, the baby, and the girl's relatives. Although there is some damage to the boy, by comparison, it is often slight. When there is a premarital pregnancy, serious and immediate decisions must be made. In reality there are no acceptable, happy, or effective solutions available. There are four possible alternatives that may be considered.

First, there is the possibility of a quick marriage. This "gives the baby a name" and may help in protecting the social reputation of the couple. But this decision often simply creates more problems. For example, in a great many cases, marriage for couples caught in these circumstances would only mean the beginning of permanent unhappiness, for their sex interest may be their only bond.

All too often the quick marriage ends either in a divorce or a long life of regret and unhappiness.

Second, there is the possibility of having the baby adopted by a married couple through legal channels. This assumes that the baby's parents would not marry. Such an alternative may be the best for all concerned. It would probably give the baby a happy home environment and understanding, loving parents. The child's real mother could move to a distant community and start life over again.

"But if she later marries happily and has other children, her love for them will bring her an awareness of the one that had to be given away. The finer her children, the more painful will be the thought of her first-born whom she was not able to know."[1]

Third, there is the possibility of an abortion. But abortion is an operation involving major problems, even when it is performed by skilled doctors. It is expensive and often dangerous, especially when performed by quacks. In most states it is illegal except under extenuating circumstances. Many cultured and scholarly people believe that abortion is murder, and it is rather difficult to completely refute this contention if one follows Christian values. Certainly there are many emotional complications that follow an illegal abortion to terminate a premarital pregnancy.

Finally, there is the possibility of keeping the baby while the girl continues to live with her parents. Thus the child would grow up with his mother in the home of his grandparents. This would deny the child the right and the privilege of associating with his father. This course would also deny the child the father's last name. In most situations it would brand the child with that ugly label — "illegitimate child." Often the experience can condition the mother and the child against men, against love, against marriage, against sex, and against life itself with all of its wonderful realities.

A premarital pregnancy is a tragedy for all concerned. It is easy to shrug one's shoulders and say that the above description is overstated. But those who do shrug off the problem have never had the responsibility of helping and advising a young girl through the problems of a premarital pregnancy.

2. A second problem involved in premarital sex relations is the *possibility of contracting venereal disease.* Venereal diseases such as syphilis and gonorrhea are always a threat to those who practice sexual promiscuity.

[1] Judson T. and Mary G. Landis, *Building a Successful Marriage,* Prentice-Hall, Inc., 1953, 2nd Edition, p. 139. Used by permission.

Since the discovery of penicillin and other efficient medicines, liberal moralists have been saying that because we now can cure venereal diseases, their threat should no longer discourage sexual freedom. Facts have proven this idea to be unrealistic. In 1957 new known cases of syphilis were reduced to only 6,251 in the United States from the 32,148 in 1950. During 1958 the decline was reversed, and there has been a steady increase since. Dr. Evelyn Duvall states that "by 1958 the trend of infectious syphilis had turned upward, followed in 1960 and 1961 by 50 percent increases each year. By 1963, after five years of annual increases, there were four and one-half times as many cases as were reported in 1957, an increase of 448 percent. . . . State health departments continue to report more than twice as many cases of gonorrhea as syphilis."[2] In 1965 the American Medical Association stated that "venereal diseases have made such an 'alarming' comeback . . . that they now represent this nation's most urgent communicable-disease problem. The venereal diseases are infecting 1,100,000 Americans a year — about 3,000 a day, or two a minute. The total consists of an estimated 100,000 new cases of infectious syphilis each year and 1,000,000 cases of gonorrhea. Almost 60 percent of these victims are in their teens. Young people have not been warned about the dangers of promiscuous behavior."[3] By 1967 the new gonorrhea cases had increased to 1,200,000 each year and syphilis in excess of 100,000. More recent reports indicate that during the last three years the rates of venereal disease have continued their upward trend, and there seems to be no end in sight. It is nonsense for any person to advocate that there is no longer any danger of premarital sexual promiscuity resulting in venereal disease.

It is true that medical science can cure venereal dis-

[2] Evelyn Millis Duvall, *Why Wait Till Marriage?*, Association Press, 1965, p. 55. Used by permission.
[3] John Troan, *Knoxville News-Sentinel*, September 1, 1965.

ease if the remedies are applied soon after the disease is contracted. The sooner the remedy is applied, the better. However, it is necessary to be realistic and say that penicillin and other medicines are not enough to control these diseases. What we must do is to control human behavior. Society must marshall all its forces (doctors, social workers, clergy, judges, police, and every other official, and the citizenry as well) and organize against this killer. It is naive to assume that some legal or welfare organization can wipe out venereal disease. Dr. Evelyn Duvall is coming to grips with reality when she says, "Premarital chastity and postmarital fidelity still remain the best safeguards against the dangers of venereal infection."[4]

3. Premarital sex relations have a *detrimental effect upon the attitudes and ideas of youth about the nature of sex.* Before premarital experimentation, young people usually think of sex as something wonderful to be anticipated. They dream about perfect sexual fulfillment in their future marriage. This is a normal and healthy attitude toward sex life. But *premarital experimentation often destroys this wholesome approach.* First sexual experiences are notoriously unsuccessful. Also, they are intensely impressive. Usually they are one-sided affairs in which the girl reluctantly yields while the boy awkwardly and hastily satisfies his own selfish desires. The mutuality of the relationship is almost non-existent. The experience is neither satisfying nor pleasant to the girl (as she usually experiences some pain) and leaves her disappointed. She feels there is something wrong with her. Her previous dreams are now shattered. Often the boy senses her disappointment and secretly feels that he is not a real man. Guilt feelings make them both miserable for days and sometimes for years. Actually, there is nothing wrong sexually with either the girl or the boy. Their problem is simply that two people just cannot find sexual fulfillment in such a situation.

[4] Duvall, *Why Wait Till Marriage?*, p. 55.

4. The smiting of conscience and the *guilt feelings that follow premarital experimentation tend to erode and destroy the courtship interest of a couple.* Our conscience is our personal inner acceptance of the norms and standards of a society. When we violate or are tempted to violate those standards, we have feelings of guilt. Conscience is a basic part of human nature that is not present in the nature of animals. Conscience and guilt feelings are a necessary and integral part of the mental and emotional life of all people. When a child has been taught for twenty years that stealing is wrong, he accepts the idea as valid and good. He makes it a part of his inner moral system. If such a youth should steal something, it is reasonable to say that he would have major guilt feelings.

In a similar manner, let us consider the case of an ordinary boy and girl who have grown up in good Christian homes. They are taught from childhood that sex belongs to marriage. Their parents, school teachers, Sunday school teachers, pastors, and friends advocate the controlling of sex until marriage. They read the Bible and find that it teaches sexual self-control. Across the years they gradually accept these ideas about sex as being true. These ideas take root and grow. They become a part of their inner value systems. Now let us assume that during courtship this young couple is caught off guard in a tempting situation. It is not willful or planned, but suddenly it happens. More accurately — they allow it to happen. It is naive rationalization to call this experience an accident. It is realistic to say that a couple simply cannot do this without punishment from within themselves. Ideas built up over many years do not vanish overnight when they are violated. Immediately thereafter their consciences strike them with terrific emotional pressure.

Thus, the guilt feelings which follow sexual experimentation tend to undermine and destroy a couple's courtship interests. They begin to find fault with each other, blame each other, and gradually drift apart. Premarital sex relations tend to separate and to destroy relationships.

5. Premarital sex relations *promote distrust, fear, and suspicion.* On the other hand, premarital self-control promotes faith, trust, and confidence, the characteristics necessary for successful courtship and marriage. After premarital intercourse, guilt feelings drive a couple to suspect each other. The boy may reason, *If she yielded to me, she may have yielded to others,* and the girl will have reason to suspect and distrust the boy.

Let us imagine that a young couple have been dating casually. After a few social dates, John persistently makes advances, and finally Mary yields. Later, Mary may fear that John will tell others of their experience and ruin her chances for a good marriage. His aggressiveness may cause her to conclude that he had been promiscuous with others. She may reason that if he insists on violating the Christian ideals before marriage, he would be just as likely to violate them after marriage. This blocks her interest in John.

Let us suppose that later Mary does marry John. Across the years it may be difficult for her to control her distrust of him. In marriage there are many times when husband and wife cannot have sex relations, such as the period during and after a pregnancy, during illnesses, military service, and other necessary separations. During these times, especially when circumstances require them to be spatially separated, the knowledge of John's premarital behavior may cause Mary to be suspicious of his present behavior. She may doubt her husband even though she does not want to do so.

To continue the illustration, let us suppose that Mary does not marry John; after she was intimate with him two or three times, they drifted apart. John went into the military service, and after two years, Mary married someone else. When John returns from service to Mary's community four years later, he may visit some of his old buddies in the local tavern. During the evening as he is being brought up to date about people and community happenings he may ask: "What ever happened to Mary Jones?" He is told that she married a certain fellow about two years before, and that they seem to have a fine marriage. At this point John laughs loudly and says: "I used to make her whenever I wanted to. She was easy!" What if a close friend of Mary's husband is present and later tells him about the episode? Just suppose! Similar experiences have happened many times. Premarital sex relations promote suspicion, distrust, and fear. Sexual self-control before marriage promotes confidence, faith, and trust.

6. Premarital sex is *motivated by characteristics that are unstable, unsocial, and often neurotic.* Such behavior shows immaturity, insecurity, lack of Christian respect for others, and a lack of concern for the other finer values of life. A person's ideas about sex are an excellent index to what the person is like in his beliefs, his values, and his personality. This is especially true of boys who attempt to force their advances on reluctant girls. In courtship young people must be concerned about the characteristics of their potential marriage partners. When a girl has refused a boy's advances, often a boy may reply: "Why don't you prove your love? You don't love me or you would." This behavior reveals a mountain of truth about such a boy. He is pure bluff and threat. He is concerned about a sexual release, not love. A girl may be sure that such a boy is selfish and immature, a bully who does not really love her. Love does not bluff or threaten or force. If a boy loves a girl, he has concern and affection for her. He will respect her body and her person. Real love is tender and makes one willing to deny himself for the loved one. A true love will respect the girl's rights, her beliefs, and her ideals.

7. Premarital sex relations *spoil the significance of the honeymoon and reduce its meaning to hollow empti-*

ness. Of the many good American social customs that have emerged in the past fifty years, the modern honeymoon is one of the better ones. The honeymoon as a social institution sustains, supplements, and completes the social, legal, and spiritual significance of the marriage ceremony; whereas the license and the marriage ceremony make the marriage socially and legally acceptable, the honeymoon transforms these symbolic rituals into a "one flesh" reality. If the wedding ceremony with all of its related activities has not been too strenuous, and if the couple has received thorough counseling on both the spiritual and sexual levels, the honeymoon can be a most meaningful and enjoyable experience.

Young people in our society rightly look forward to moving out of the state of singleness into the state of marriage. This involves many changes in their lives — their separate ambitions, feelings, and beliefs must be merged with those of another person. Although many different types of marriage adjustments are begun on the honeymoon, it is realistic to say that one of the most important purposes of the honeymoon is to provide a private and relaxed atmosphere for the couple's first sex experiences. But when there has been premarital sexual experimentation, a honeymoon becomes rather meaningless. One is not surprised that a study by sociologists Kanin and Howard revealed that out of 177 couples studied, 87 percent of the couples who had not had premarital sexual intercourse had a honeymoon, as compared to only 47 percent of those couples who had had premarital intercourse.[5]

Of course, it takes a much longer period than an average honeymoon to achieve a thorough and efficient sexual adjustment. Yet, even though the sexual progress during the few short days of the honeymoon may be rather limited, the memory of an enjoyable honeymoon is a spiritual treasure too valuable to miss.

[5] Eugene J. Kanin and David H. Howard, *American Sociological Review,* 23:5, 558.

8. *To wait until marriage for sex relations has the advantage of the couple learning together.* Sexual adjustment in marriage involves much time, patience, and understanding. It is one of the most complex and most personal of all human relationships. For a couple to learn sexual adjustment together after marriage can be one of the most beautiful and most meaningful experiences that they will ever encounter in their lives. Learning together to respond to each other's needs in tenderness brings not only a new dimension to the sex experience itself, but to the inner self-confidence and security of both partners and to the marriage as a whole. The working out together of a good sexual adjustment after marriage gives support to the ego of each of the partners. It builds trust and confidence, and it is one of the major positive elements contributing to the well-being of the married couple which results in two well-integrated "one flesh" personalities. Learning together after marriage is the will of God. It is the ultimate in human love.

9. Finally, there is much evidence that *sexual self-control until marriage works.* It produces happy marriages. On the other hand, there is much evidence that premarital sexual permissiveness does not work. The couple lives under the shadow of a secret and a two-way suspicion. Often those who are permissive before marriage tend to be permissive after marriage. Premarital permissiveness is the real cause of many divorces, even though it is not stated in the official divorce documents. Marriage counselors have much confidential information to this effect in their files.

Dr. Norman Vincent Peale says, "In my forty-odd years as a minister I have counseled with literally hundreds of men and women who have kept searching for sex satisfaction with one partner after another, and my sober conclusion is this: If it is depth of emotion that you are looking for in love making, or even the maximum degree of physical sensation, you cannot disperse your emotional and physical energies, or divide and dilute them. You must concentrate them. Sex at the right place at the right time with the right person under the right circumstances is just about the most tremendous experience human beings can know."[6] He is simply saying that sex belongs to marriage.

I checked my personal marriage counseling files and found that 76 percent of the cases involved premarital sex relations as part of the total problem of the marriage conflict. Of course, there are many and varied interlocking factors involved in marriage unhappiness and divorce, but it may be that in cases of premarital promiscuity this fact is really larger than some of us realize.

The emphasis here is that sexual control until marriage *works*. It produces personal confidence, trust, and sexual happiness. This is the major thrust of Dr. Peale's argument against premarital promiscuity. He says, "This argument that sexual restraint leads ultimately to *sexual intensity and depth* is one that many young people will accept, because it offers them a glorious plus, not a gloomy minus. It is a highly personal reward. . . . It gives . . . greater intensity of experience in this, the most intense of all experiences."[7]

In 1959 Isadore Rubin initiated a survey to measure the sexual activities of older persons.

> Six thousand questionnaires were mailed to individuals who had attained sufficient eminence in their professions to be listed in *Who's Who in America*. More than eight hundred men answered the series of questions put to them. . . . Among those replying, the largest groups consisted of educators, business leaders, attorneys, engineers, physicians, clergymen and writers.
>
> The results indicated that 70 percent of the married men in this survey (all sixty-five or over) engaged with some regularity in sexual intercourse and that the overwhelming majority of these had a generally satisfactory

[6] Norman Vincent Peale, *Sin, Sex and Self-Control*, Guideposts Associates, Inc., 1965, p. 90. Used by permission.
[7] *Ibid.*, p. 91.

sexual life. The frequency of coitus averaged one to four times a month. Even in the group of 104 men aged seventy-five to ninety-two, almost one-half reported coitus was still satisfactory, and six of these engaged in coitus more than eight times a month. . . .

Interestingly, the oldest married male who still engaged in coitus satisfactorily was a clergyman, aged ninety-two. As a group, clergymen indicated a high proportion of satisfactory coitus.[8]

For youth to fulfill their life dreams and meet their total needs, they must practice sexual self-control until marriage and then practice fidelity in marriage. This is the nature of the reality of the world in which we live.

[8] Isadore Rubin, *Sexual Life After Sixty*, Basic Books, Inc., 1965, pp. 36, 37. Used by permission.

Why Society Objects to Premarital Sex Relations

CHAPTER 5

NECKING, PETTING, AND "MAKING OUT" ON SOCIAL DATES AND DURING COURTSHIP

Let no one think little of you because you are young, but always set an example for believers, in speech, conduct, love, faith, and purity ... devote yourself to the ... reading of the Scriptures. ... Make it your habit to pay close attention to yourself and your teaching. Persevere in these things, for if you do you will save both yourself and those who listen to you.

Never reprove an older man, but always appeal to him as a father. Treat younger men like brothers, older women like mothers, younger women like sisters, with perfect purity.
(I Timothy 4:12, 13, 16; 5:1, 2, Williams)

"Oh, Sue, I just had to call and tell you the news. You'll just never believe it! You'll never!" exclaims Myra breathlessly, almost dropping the telephone receiver on the floor. "Jim asked me if I wanted to go to the basketball game with him, and mom and dad said I could go. Oh, Sue, I'm so excited! Can you imagine! He is going to come by and pick me up in his car. My *first* date! I'll just die if anything goes wrong! I'll just lay right down and die! Wish me luck, dear? Oh, Sue, I'm about to pop! I'll call ya tomorrow, O.K.? See ya! Bye!" she exclaims as she slams the phone down on the hook.

Myra is riding so high on "cloud nine" that she has just set the tone and mood for all the members of her family — excited, jittery, nervous. But for mom and dad, feelings of apprehensiveness and nostalgia arise. Myra is now fifteen years old. Their little girl has entered into a new phase of her life.

Myra has associated with boys before — at school, at church, and at group parties. But this is her first official social date. And what an exciting experience that first date will be for her, as it is for all young people. And rightly so. Yet, you young people deserve to know what this wonderful new adventure involves and what it really means.

Social dating is a casual type of dating in which a girl or boy dates a variety of individuals and does not settle down to one person exclusively. Usually the emotional involvement between a boy and girl who are "social dating" could be described by the term "like." Young people date those they like, or those who are attractive to them. During "social dating," as we are using the term, a boy and a girl are not "in love" with each other. However, when social dating with one person continues for an indefinite length of time, love may develop. When love develops in the relationship, it is no longer social dating. Thus, during the period of social dating the relationship involves a boy and girl who "like" each other. We must not overlook the major and significant difference between "like" and "love."

In high school the term "going steady" is used to describe dating when there is little or often no love involved. The relationship is for the purpose of dating security and social status. At the moment, it is generally not associated with the idea of possible marriage. On the college level, the idea of going steady usually means "we think we love each other" and "we are moving in the direction of possible marriage." Thus, much going steady in high school is really just social dating. It is in this period of social dating that the young person learns various rules of social etiquette; he/she learns to carry on an effective boy-girl conversation; and he/she learns to assume the responsibility of interpersonal social life.

He/she also learns how to cope with various kinds of individuals and is exposed to many types of personalities which will aid him/her in eventually selecting a marriage partner.

One of the major problems that plagues these early dating years is that of necking, petting, and "making out." "He's all hands!" "He's just like an octopus!" "I'm afraid if we keep on doing this, we'll just go too far!" "Sometimes we say we're going to the movies, but we don't; we just go and park and make out." These statements are heard time and time again in counseling with young people.

Since these activities do present so many problems to you young people in your social dating, let's discuss them openly and candidly. We will define the terms and examine carefully the facts involved in order to help you make an objective decision as to the rightness or wrongness of petting, necking, and "making out" on social dates.

Necking has, in the past, normally referred to embracing and kissing. The term petting may be defined as physical contact between a boy and a girl for the purpose of sexual sensation and pleasure which stops short of sexual intercourse. There are four distinct levels of intensity in petting. Moving from the mildest form to the most intense form, these are (1) holding hands, (2) putting the arms around each other's bodies outside of clothing, (3) kissing, and (4) moving the hands over each other's bodies on the inside of the clothing. Judson and Mary Landis state frankly and accurately that petting is nature's plan for sexual arousal in making "preparation for sexual intercourse"[1] in marriage.

In recent years the term "making out" has been used often by both high school and college youth. Our survey to determine the meaning of "making out" revealed that the term is used in three different ways. To some it

[1] Landis, *Building a Successful Marriage*, 2nd Edition, p. 67.

means "necking" and to some it means "petting." To others it means both necking and petting.

With these definitions of social dating, necking, petting, and "making out" in mind, let us consider the question before us. Is petting right or wrong on social dates? Let's look at the facts involved.

Dr. and Mrs. Landis state that "Girls are not so easily aroused sexually as boys are, and what seems to girls to be relatively safe petting may lead the boy beyond the point of his self-control."[2] This may cause him to force the girl when he does not really mean to do so. Also, as the Landises point out, in the process of petting on social dates, "The girl herself may be aroused to an emotional response that is new to her, and many girls mistake this new response for love."[3] The difference between sexual arousal and true love is major and significant.

Insecure girls often use petting on social dates as a device to win the boy. There is little or no evidence that this approach will succeed. Petting on social dates often lowers a couple's opinion of each other and causes them to cease their dating, when otherwise the relationship might have developed into a permanent courtship. When a girl pets on social dates, this information has a way of getting around to other boys. A boy who is interested in a girl only because she pets on dates is really only interested in himself. He will cease dating her when he meets a more attractive girl who will pet. That boys do not choose girls who are sexually promiscuous to be their wives is supported by research. When most boys marry, they want a girl with inner character, high ideals, and personal self-control.

Often young people try to distinguish between acceptable and unacceptable petting. Holding hands and "relatively unstimulating kissing and embracing" (the first three levels defined above) are said by some mod-

2 *Ibid.,* p. 67.
3 *Ibid.,* p. 67.

ern youth to be acceptable. The more extreme forms of petting (movement of the hands over the body inside clothing) are said to be unacceptable. I am frankly suspicious of the phrase "relatively unstimulating kissing and embracing." If we are going to face truth unequivocally — and face truth we must — it is necessary to state bluntly that there is no such thing as unstimulating kissing and embracing.

Imagine a handsome, eighteen-year-old boy and a beautiful, sixteen-year-old girl in some isolated spot kissing and embracing. How could this experience not be stimulating sexually? We must be completely honest. Kissing and embracing *are* sexually stimulating — God made human nature to be this way. It is a short step from kissing and embracing to other forms of sexual stimulation. An aroused sexual feeling is hard to control, and the more intense the stimulation, the more difficult it is to control. Continued sexual stimulation creates a determined biological compulsion to go on and on. Many young people do not have the mature iron will necessary to call a halt to this process, and many seemingly mature youth do yield to these forces, even though they do not mean to yield and have boldly assured themselves that they will not. During sexual excitement, maturity, intelligence, and moral and religious considerations are often temporarily overpowered, suspended, or rendered ineffective.

Let's face it, many young couples (who have insisted that a little petting on social dates is normal and harmless) go all the way. Afterwards the young people involved are overpowered with guilt feelings. Their consciences strike them like the blows of a giant sledge hammer. Petting on social dates is the basic cause of many premarital pregnancies. When sex gets out of hand during social dating, many young people become conditioned against sex and develop emotional problems and unhealthy attitudes about sex, marriage, and life. We must face the truth, the honest facts, and be completely realistic. Kissing and embracing *are* sexually stimulating.

Let me ask a simple question: What is the purpose of petting on social dates? Remember, in social dating the couple is not in love and has no plans at this time to marry. Then why pet? Although those who advocate petting on social dates are reluctant to admit it, obviously the correct answer is that it is for the purpose of the physical pleasure of sexual stimulation — to satisfy the desires of the moment and to enjoy this sexual stimulation as an end in itself. This type of motivation is selfish. It is a flagrant violation of the principles inherent in the creative plan of God. The persons involved violate each other, their own selves, and the plan and will of God.

Finally, necking and petting on social dates are a violation of the general teaching of the Scriptures. Paul in his letter to the Ephesians discusses (in chapters four and five) the moral and spiritual virtues that a Christian should cultivate, and the sins and vices they should avoid. These chapters are concerned with right and wrong sexual practices. Paul says,

> This is my instruction, then, which I give you from the Lord. Do not live any longer as the gentiles live. For they live blindfold in a world of illusion, and are cut off from the life of God through ignorance and insensitiveness. They have stifled their consciences and then surrendered themselves to sensuality, practising any form of impurity which lust can suggest. But you have learned nothing like that from Christ, if you have really heard his voice and understood the truth that Jesus has taught you.
> *(Ephesians 4:17-21, Phillips)*

From this passage we may assume that Christian youth should avoid petting on social dates because such activity amounts to "surrendering (oneself) to sensuality," allowing lust to lead to the practice of impurity and vice, and to violating the will of Christ.

Further, we may assume that Paul's moral instructions to the young preacher, Timothy, should apply to all

Christian youth everywhere. In I Timothy 5:22 (Phillips) Paul says, "Be careful that your own life is pure."

By this time it is obvious that those young people whose major interest in social dating is sex are confused, immature, probably insecure, and may be emotionally ill. They have been misinformed and misled by the delinquent adults of our society. They do not understand sex well enough to accept it as a normal and wonderful part of total life that God intended it to be.

The sexual act does not produce love, but is a medium for expressing love that is already present — the love between husband and wife. Sexual experimentation without love is cheap and destroys a relationship. To violate or destroy another person to satisfy a particular feeling or urge which will last only a few minutes is expensive indeed. The stakes are high and the rewards are low. It is really not worth the risks which have to be taken.

We are now ready to move from the period that we have called social dating to discuss the periods of courtship called "going steady," engaged-to-be-engaged, and engagement. The question before us is: "What about necking, petting, and 'making out' during the later stages of courtship?" Or, to restate the question: "What should be the pattern of love and affection of a couple insofar as physical bodily contact is concerned during the periods of 'going steady,' engaged-to-be-engaged, and engagement?"

Brief definitions of these three periods of courtship are in order. "Going steady," in the proper sense of the term, refers to the period when a mature boy or girl has settled down to dating one particular person. The difference between social dating and "going steady" is that the couple "going steady" thinks they are in love with each other and are in the process of genuinely testing this love. They are so concerned about each other that they do not want to date anyone else. Usually they have a private understanding that they will be faithful to each other and will not date anyone else. The process of "going steady" may continue for weeks and months. If the couple decides that they are not a good marriage risk and that they do not really love each other, they break up. On the other hand, if during the process of "going steady" they gradually decide that their love for each other is *beyond all doubt* genuine, and that they are a good marriage risk, they usually move into a courtship relationship called "engaged-to-be-engaged." This means that across the weeks and months the couple gradually talks about planning their lives together until they come to a tentative private understanding about possible marriage. The understanding is temporary. It is not finalized or binding. The relationship is usually not made public at this point, yet it constitutes a step in real plans toward marriage.

I personally like this new step in the process of courtship for two reasons. First, it brings the girl into the total process of the planning from the very beginning. It is a two-way conversation and communication between the couple about planning their lives together. The boy and the girl are equal in the planning. This does away with the old idea that in courtship the girl must be completely passive and wait coyly for the young man to propose. Secondly, the engaged-to-be-engaged period is a buffer zone: it gives the couple more time for making sure that their personalities make a good marriage risk and that their love is genuine and enduring. During this period the couple has time to work out any doubtful matters and uncertainties concerning their possible marriage.

The final step in courtship is engagement. The engaged-to-be-engaged couple makes a final decision about their marriage. In continuing to plan their lives together, the tentative plans for marriage become finalized. There is often no proposal, nor is there need for one. A date is set, and plans for the wedding begin to materialize.

With these definitions before us, we are now ready to discuss the question, "What should be the pattern of love and affection of a couple insofar as physical contact is concerned during the periods of 'going steady,' engaged-to-be-engaged, and engagement?" It is important to note that the difference between social dating and these later stages of courtship is that a couple *thinks they are in love* or is *certain that they are in love* during "going steady," engaged-to-be-engaged, and engagement. Usually they are developed enough in mental, emotional, spiritual, and economic maturity to shoulder the responsibilities of marriage. These are major and significant differences.

It is natural and Christian that such couples should express their love to each other. Our problem is just what part should bodily contact play in this love expression during these three periods of courtship. I want to submit the proposition that a limited and controlled amount of bodily contact for the purpose of love expression is *natural and Christian*. I would suggest four guidelines: (1) the proper time, (2) the proper place, (3) the proper understanding, and (4) the proper restraint. By proper time and place, I do not refer to a love-making couple sitting on a public bench in the shade of a tree on a high school or college campus at midday, while dozens of students are passing to and fro on their way to the library, classes, or the cafeteria. Some of the excessive public behavior of a few immature couples on high school and college campuses is extremely embarrassing to the administration, the faculty, and most students. This behavior is disrespectful, crude, and vulgar.

We need to learn that true love is personal, that love demands privacy, and that love loses something when it has an audience. I suspect this kind of "public love-making" for what it really is, "sex as an end-in-itself." I suspect it as being lust and not love.

"Proper understanding" means that the couple understands that the kiss is a personal, limited expression of love, and not sex as an end-in-itself. A couple must be realistic and admit that kissing arouses sexual emotions, and, therefore, this type of love expression must be bounded by intelligent limitations that are thoroughly understood and accepted by both.

"Proper restraint" does not mean two hours of heavy petting while parked in some secret spot or at a drive-in theater. Rather, it refers to the couple (both boy and girl) using an iron will to stay within the intelligent limitations and boundary lines agreed upon through their mutual understanding.

At the proper time and place, and with the proper understanding and restraint, it is normal, it is natural, it is good, it is Christian for mature couples, in the last stages of courtship, to express their love to each other by limited bodily contact. It is within the framework of basic Christian principles and ideals. I recommend it. To do otherwise is unrealistic. To insist that mature couples wait until marriage before they kiss is downright ridiculous. However, this extreme is not nearly so ridiculous as the other extreme that promotes and demands sexual permissiveness in courtship from the early teens onward.

Expression of love during the courtship period calls for self-control, self-discipline, and respect for one's sweetheart. Every premarriage and marriage counselor of youth has observed that when Christian respect and restraint are not practiced during courtship, the whole framework and fabric of love tends to decline, decay, and disintegrate into lust. Respect, restraint, and self-control are a part of love and are basic foundation stones of Christian behavior and personality.

CHAPTER 6

SOME QUESTIONS ABOUT SEX EXAMINED

Cursed be the social wants that sin against the strength of
   youth!
Cursed be the social lies that warp us from the living truth!
Cursed be the sickly forms that err from honest Nature's rule!
Cursed be the gold that gilds the straiten'd forehead of the
   fool!

Tennyson, *Locksley Hall*

To sin by silence when they should protest makes cowards
out of men. Abraham Lincoln

Many erroneous ideas about sex are promoted in our
culture. Some are stated openly through literature de-
fending premarital sex relations. Others are superstitions
on the level of old wives' tales. All need to be exposed.
These ideas have little or no substance in reality, yet
many times they are unthinkingly repeated in the presence of young people, and the young generation accepts
these ideas as facts. Our youth should know the truth
concerning the widely held false beliefs and superstitions about sex. Knowing the truth, modern young people can more effectively plan a program of sexual self-
control until marriage. In this chapter we will examine
ten of these false ideas.

1. *Are some women sexually frigid?* By the term "frigid" we mean cold sexually by nature, incapable of response, and unable to experience or enjoy normal sex

life in marriage. It is often implied that God created some women like this and there is nothing that can be done about it. Actually, there is no such thing as a woman frigid by nature. It is true that there are many women who have been taught, directly or indirectly, that sex is something evil. They think of sex as being necessary only for reproduction. Otherwise, they think sexual relations are rather sinful. When a woman with this attitude marries, of course she does not respond normally in sexual experiences with her husband. A woman who thinks sex is sinful cannot have a normal sex life in marriage. Somewhere in her marriage experience her husband may refer to her as being "frigid" or as "cold as an iceberg." Her main problem is that she is guided by false and unchristian ideas. Once she can replace these with the normal Christian ideas about sex, she can then gradually learn to adjust and to enjoy a normal, happy sex life in marriage.

There are other young women who are simply uneducated about the nature of sex. They enter marriage knowing little about their own sexual nature and their young husband often knows even less. Their sex life ultimately becomes an upsetting, difficult affair, a blind trial-and-error experience. Under these conditions the young wife simply does not experience normal sexual expression, but she is not frigid. The couple's problem is that both are ignorant as to the nature of female sexuality. Once they become enlightened they can gradually develop a normal sexual adjustment in their marriage.

2. *Is the male more sexual than the female?* This idea is usually assumed to be true because the time required for a man's sexual arousal is much less than the time needed for a woman's arousal. But we cannot measure sexuality by the speed in sexual timing. An honest comparison of male and female as to which is the more sexual would have to include a comparison of the total nature of sexuality of both male and female. When we

Some Questions About Sex Examined

look at the complete picture, the concept that the male is more sexual vanishes. Two facts will substantiate this statement. First, in marriage the husband can have only one sexual orgasm during a sexual experience. Some length of time must pass (several hours, or even a few days) before he can normally have a second sexual orgasm. On the other hand, his wife may learn in marriage to have several orgasms — one after another — in one period of ten or twenty minutes. Secondly, our research with 151 young married couples showed that if a couple could have a sexual experience including orgasm whenever they wished, every 2.7 days would be sufficient for the man and 3.2 days for the woman. Out of the 151 wives who answered, 40 percent stated that they would like to have sex relations as often as their husbands, and 10 percent of the wives stated that they would like to have sex relations more often than their husbands. Thus, when all the facts are considered, it becomes necessary for us to reject the idea that man is more sexual than woman. Yet, neither are we trying to say that woman is more sexual than man. We are stating that although God created men and women with some differences, they are really equal sexually. When they follow Christian procedures in their marriage, they complement and supplement each other. They each experience fulfillment. It is of utmost importance that both bride and groom go into a marriage relationship with the idea that God created them as sexual equals.

3. *Does a woman's body shape affect her sexual capacity?* For years the money-minded mass media, especially the Hollywood movie industry, has been saying by implication and innuendos that only women with a certain size and shape are really "sexy." Thus 36-24-36 has become a false sex-symbol. Unfortunately, many men and women seem to have believed this naive propaganda completely. This is one of the most fantastic lies that has ever been accepted by the seemingly educated, but gullible public.

This false 36-24-36 idea is largely an invention of men and not of women. First, it is promoted by immoral, corrupt, licentious men who are interested largely in satisfying selfishly their own egocentric sex drives. Secondly, it is supported by greedy men who promote sexual permissiveness for the purposes of vested interests; that is, to cash in on the human sex drive and use it to make money, as many do through the mass media.

We do not mean to say or imply that a boy or girl, in selecting a marriage partner, should not consider the size or shape of his or her body. But certainly this should be one of the last and minor considerations in the selection.

To say that only girls with certain body measurements can be sexy is about as intelligent as saying that all girls who are over six feet tall or under five feet tall have weak, inefficient digestive and respiratory systems. Or it is about as sensible as saying that the color of a woman's hair or skin would determine her sexual efficiency in marriage. The size and shape of a person's body has little or nothing to do with his or her sexuality. The only exception to this is when a person becomes excessively overweight. In these cases, available energy is consumed in carrying excess body weight, and thus such people may have less energy for a normal sex life. The real tools necessary for a satisfying sex life in marriage lie within a woman's (and a man's) mind. They are non-physical characteristics. They are such Christian qualities as character, honesty, love, concern, fidelity, trust, thoughtfulness, tenderness, understanding, cooperation, and a balanced sex education.

There is much evidence that many young women, especially during the teens, worry about being flat-chested, that is, having small breasts. Their worry is really caused by the false idea that girls with large breasts are more "sexy." The facts are (1) that such a girl is still young, (2) that as she grows to adulthood and older, her breasts will grow larger and be normal for her, and (3) that the size of a woman's breasts has little or nothing to do with normal sexual efficiency in marriage.

4. *Is sex just a game?* Popular among some of the young generation today, especially with the so-called "in" college crowd, is the "live-in," "love-in," and "bed-up" type of relationships between single men and women students. On the upsurge, too, among many married couples are key club parties where the center of fun and games has become the swapping of spouses for the purpose of sexual intercourse. Ultimately then, to these people, sex has become a game. They have developed a philosophy that sex is fun and just a game; and they defend this philosophy in sexy articles in many pornographic magazines.

Certainly this description of the sexual relationship is directly opposite the plan of the Creator for sexual intercourse in marriage. God's plan involves two people in absolute cooperation. The rules followed are of divine origin (I Corinthians 7:2-5) and are not man-made. Each participant is not concerned about his own selfish gratification but seeks to meet the sexual needs of the other. Both parties are honored with personal happiness, and there is no sadness or humiliation.

Sex as fun or a game involves major risks, guilt feelings, and emotional problems. It violates divine rules. It would be unrealistic to imply that there is no physical or emotional pleasure in sexual promiscuity. But the Christian prefers to follow self-control with God's people rather than to enjoy even a few fleeting pleasures of sin for a short season (Hebrews 11:25).

5. *Is sex as normal as breathing, eating, and drinking?* Often the advocates of sexual permissiveness answer "Yes" to youth and defend the idea vigorously. This "nature" idea is appealing to youth. In fact, it appeals to all of us. And, there is much truth here. Sex is natural. It is true that sex is as normal a part of creation as breathing oxygen, eating food, or drinking water. In this

respect these experiences are alike. However, the permissive thinkers fail to point out the *differences* between human sex life and our consumption of oxygen, food, and water.

Dr. Sylvanus M. Duvall points out three major differences between sex hunger and other hungers such as hunger for food and drink.[1] We summarize his three points as follows:

(1) The denial of sexual satisfaction in life does not produce harmful physical effects. Those people who do not eat food or drink water will weaken physically and die. For a man or woman to go through life without having sexual intercourse produces no comparable physical harm. A man with his strong sex drive who never has sexual intercourse can find physically necessary relief in nocturnal emissions.

(2) The satisfaction of hunger for food and thirst for drink need have no social consequences as does sexual intercourse. A person's selection and eating of food and drink can be largely a private matter and have no social significance for society as a whole. On the other hand, satisfying the sex hunger through promiscuous sexual intercourse has major social consequences. There is the possibility of venereal disease and pregnancy. Society is rightly concerned about both of these and must, therefore, have some moral codes. Even if we have the know-how to control both, we will still need moral codes because of the human factor involved. Those who assume the least responsibility for the proper development of children also assume the least responsibility for having them, whether within or outside the marriage relationship.

(3) Satisfying the sex hunger in sexual intercourse involves another person or persons. The food and drink that a man consumes may be prepared by someone else and brought to him by a waitress. Such services rarely

[1] Sylvanus M. Duvall, *Men, Women, and Morals,* Association Press, 1952, pp. 37, 38.

result in any serious personal involvement. These services are in an entirely different category from satisfaction of the sexual hunger derived directly from the body of another person.

Therefore, Dr. Duvall concludes that the idea that sex hunger "is *like any other hunger* is nonsense."[2]

6. *Does following Christian principles and living a consecrated Christian life block good sex life in marriage?* There are three lines of thought that may throw light on this question. In the first place, it is our opinion that basic Christian principles are conducive to good sex life. In human interpersonal relationships, Christianity teaches 1) that worth and values reside in persons and not in animals or things, 2) that we should have respect for the rights of all persons, 3) that we should be characterized by unselfish sacrifice, 4) that we should show kindness and understanding toward others, 5) that we should be tolerant, slow to judge or criticize, 6) that we should be concerned about the happiness and well-being of others, 7) that we should bear one another's burdens, and 8) that we should practice self-discipline and self-control. It is immediately obvious that these Christian concepts are the foundation principles necessary for good sexual adjustment.

On the other hand, there are certain human traits that tend to block good sex life, such as 1) selfishness, 2) impatience, 3) unconcern for the needs and rights of others, 4) quickness to blame or to condemn, 5) unwillingness to learn, and 6) the determination to satisfy the desires of the moment. It is immediately obvious that these are non-Christian traits. Truly it can be said that basic Christian ideals are the key to both a happy marriage and a satisfying sex life.

In the second place, our research seems to indicate that Christianity tends to make possible good sexual adjustment in marriage. Out of the 151 couples in our study, 98 percent were church members, 83 percent of

[2] *Ibid.*, p. 37.

husbands and 96 percent of wives had attended Sunday school regularly in childhood and youth, 76 percent of husbands and 79 percent of wives had been Sunday school teachers, 73 percent had regularly given a tenth of their income into their church, 86 percent read from the Bible and prayed audibly together on their wedding night, 90 percent practiced regular family worship, 90 percent had prayer before meals, and 96 percent of husbands and 93 percent of wives led public prayer in church activities.[3]

It is probably safe to generalize that 90 to 95 percent of the members of the sample were active, consecrated Christian individuals. Let us point out that in the marriage of these Christian couples, 78 percent adjusted sexually within a week, 12 percent adjusted in two months, while 6 percent had adjusted only at the end of thirty months. After the couples had been married six months to one year, 96 percent of the women who had adjusted sexually stated that their attempts to experience orgasm succeeded all of the time or most of the time. Also, during this same period, 41 percent of the couples indicated that husband and wife had orgasms together all of the time or most of the time, and 38 percent had orgasms together some of the time.[4] This rate of adjustment is superior to the adjustment rate of other studies. If living a Christian life tends to block good sexual adjustment in marriage, how do we explain the high rate of adjustment of the members of our study? Of course, we must not overlook the fact that there are many complex factors involved in good sexual adjustment in marriage. Most of the couples in our research had from two to four years of college education and were continuing their education after marriage. All of the couples received detailed premarital counseling. These two factors alone are pertinent in understanding the high rate of sexual adjustment indicated by the

[3] Miles, Herbert J., *Sexual Happiness in Marriage,* Appendix I, p. 131.
[4] *Ibid.,* p. 131; Appendix II, pp. 132-146.

sample. Although we cannot be positive, there seems to be a relation in our study between Christian values and motivations and sexual adjustment in marriage. There is certainly no evidence here that Christian values and motivations block good sexual adjustment.

Some writers, critical of Christianity, imply that young people committed to Christian ideals cannot talk objectively about sex in planning marriage. Our research indicates that this theory is false. Ninety-one percent of the couples revealed that they "discussed frankly together personal attitudes and rather complete details about sex" before their marriage. Ninety-seven percent had so discussed sex one month before marriage.

In the third place, often many false ideas about sex are charged to Christianity when these ideas are really opposite of the Judeo-Christian teaching about sex. To illustrate, a couple both thirty years old, the parents of three children, were separated and about to secure a divorce. Mrs. X, the mother of the wife, visited the family pastor to request his help in avoiding the divorce. In exploring the possible causes of the conflict between the couple, the pastor finally inquired if the couple had been having a normal sex life. Mrs. X was indignant and said, "Sir, I'll have you know that the X's are Christians. When my children were born, I stopped sleeping with my husband (meaning they stopped having sexual intercourse) and have not slept with him since. When my daughter's third child was born, I instructed her to stop sleeping with her husband. She has not slept with him in five years. Sir, I'll have you know that all this talk about sex is beneath the dignity of the Christian life." The couple divorced.

Any enlightened person knows that the ideas of Mrs. X were perverted and unchristian. To hold Christianity responsible for Mrs. X's ideas is like holding medical science responsible for the many naive beliefs people have about the cause and cure of diseases.

7. *Has Christianity always opposed sex?* Many ill-in-

formed people who know little or nothing about Christianity have the habit of saying glibly and with hostile sarcasm that the *Christian religion has always opposed sex as being evil.* Many innocent people who are inexperienced as Christians accept this idea as truth, when the statement is completely false. It was Jehovah God who created the human race — male and female (Genesis 1:27). After their creation, the Creator gave them instructions as to their future relationships. He said, "Therefore shall a man leave his father and his mother, and shall cleave unto his wife: and they shall be *one flesh.* And *they were both naked,* the man and his wife, and *were not ashamed"* (Genesis 2:24 — italics added). Doubtless the term "one flesh" had varied shades of meaning in the instructions of the Creator, but it is obvious that the central core meaning was that in marriage husband and wife should have sexual intercourse and that it should be a personal pleasure of which they should not be ashamed. In other passages in the Old Testament sexual intercourse in marriage is described as the normal method to use in meeting the sexual needs of husband and wife — for example, Proverbs 5:15-19 and the Song of Solomon 2:6 and 8:3. It is well to remember that these passages do not refer to reproduction.

In the New Testament, Jesus, early in His ministry, attended and participated in a wedding in Cana of Galilee, and thus He sanctioned marriage, including its sexual relationships (John 2:1-11). Later, when the Pharisees questioned Jesus about divorce, He repeated word for word the Genesis account of man and woman leaving their parents to join in a marriage, a one-flesh relationship (Matthew 19:3-6 and Mark 10:6-9). He reminded the Pharisees that "from the beginning of creation" the sexual one-flesh relationship had been the plan of God for man and woman in marriage. Other New Testament writers follow this same interpretation of the sexual relationship in marriage (Paul in I Corinthians 7:2-5, I

Thessalonians 4:1-8, and the writer of Hebrews in Hebrews 13:4).

After the close of the New Testament period, the idea that sex is evil crept into the Early Church and caused many problems on through the Middle Ages, influenced by the thinking of such men as Mani of Persia (A.D. 215), Augustine (A.D. 354-430), and Thomas Aquinas (A.D. 1225-1274). Other early churchmen, such as Jerome, Peter Abelard, and John Chrysostom considered the body evil and sex sinful.[5]

As Martin Luther matured as a Reformation leader, he defended sex in marriage as being good, both by his actions and by his teachings. He left the monastery, married at the age of forty-two, and had three children. "Of the thirty years of his literary activity more than twenty were spent in the environment of a happy marriage."[6] In general Luther taught that "the body was made as something good ... marriage ... is acceptable unto God. Man is indeed obliged to marry for the simple reason that in creation God commanded him to do so. God created man with such a strong sexual urge that man is left with no choice. His desire for gratification with the opposite sex is as natural as the flame that consumes the straw when it is kindled by fire. Sexual desire is as necessary and as important as hunger and thirst."[7] Further, Luther not only refused to condemn sex and marriage, but he also insisted on bringing both under divine grace by directing man's look at Christ. "You cannot sanctify sex by abstinence," he argued, "nor can you sanctify marriage by making it a sacrament. Both can be sanctified only by God's grace."[8]

Oscar E. Feucht and the Lutheran scholars who wrote *Sex and the Church* describe many post-Reformation

[5] Letha Scanzoni, *Sex and the Single Eye*, Zondervan, 1968. Used by permission.
[6] Oscar E. Feucht, Editor, *Sex and the Church*, Concordia Publishing House, 1961, p. 84.
[7] *Ibid.*, pp. 77-78.
[8] *Ibid.*, p. 85.

Christian scholars during the sixteenth to the eighteenth centuries who rejected the idea that sex is evil and stated specifically that sex was created by the Creator and was a positive good.[9]

Adolph von Harless, writing as late as 1875, described sex in marriage as good and within the framework of Biblical and Christian evangelical teaching. Dr. Feucht quotes von Harless as follows:

> Where the attraction between two persons of opposite sex is purely a matter of mind and not an attraction of both body and mind, there is no motive for contracting a marriage. Christian marriage ... is the flowing together of two lives and the surrender of the whole person, one to the other. ... The Christian cannot accept the pagan notion that the body (flesh) and matter are evil while the mind and things of the spirit alone are good. God does not order the killing of the life of the body, but sin. In fact God wants us to love the body of this flesh (Ephesians 5:29). The battle is not against the flesh but against sin ... so that the reborn man may glorify God in body as well as spirit (Romans 6:12, 13). In Christian thinking the body is neither despised nor idealized (as among the heathen), but it is held to be holy, consecrated to God as His temple (I Corinthians 6:15, 19, 20).[10]

During the last hundred years hundreds of Christian scholars have stated thousands of times, through both the spoken and written word, that the Creator-God created sex for marriage as a positive good. Neither the Old Testament nor the New Testament teaches that sex is evil.

Perhaps you are asking, "What is this I have been hearing from my parents and my church all of my life about sex being evil?" The answer is that you have heard them saying "The misuse and abuse of sex is

[9] These scholars include Friedrich Baldwin (1575-1627), Martin Chemnitz (1522-1586), John Gerhard (1582-1637), J. F. Koenig (1619-1664), Johann Andreas Quenstedt (1617-1685), John Williams Baier (1647-1697), David Hollaz (1648-1713), and Adolph von Harless (1806-1879).

[10] Feucht, pp. 102-103.

evil." They have been saying that "Sexual intercourse before marriage (fornication) is evil." They have been saying that "Sexual intercourse by a married person with someone other than his or her husband or wife (adultery) is evil."

In light of the above factual evidence, it is difficult to understand how any person can state that Christianity has always opposed sex as being evil. The statement is deceptive, dishonest, and false. I would be the first to admit, however, that our parents and our churches have been so busy stating the negative aspects of sex that they have failed to come through clearly to youth with the positive message that sex is good in the plan of our Creator.

8. *Do primitive people have any moral codes?* Another false idea about sex that has been popular with uninformed people is that *primitive people have no sexual moral codes.* It is pointed out that many of them wear little or no clothing. It is assumed that people who wear little or no clothing are sexually permissive. The argument is usually ended with such statements as: "Their culture has survived, and they seem to live a happy, simple life. Why can't we get rid of our moral rules about sex like these primitive people?" These false ideas are often strengthened and promoted by radical newspaper, magazine, and movie writers who make sensational references to widespread sexual promiscuity among primitive people.

During the last hundred years anthropologists have studied rather thoroughly and scientifically the social and cultural behavior patterns of most primitive tribes on the earth. Arnold W. Green discusses the universal features of the family organization of primitive people as observed by modern anthropologists. Some of his observations are as follows:

(1) All societies approve of certain forms of sexual ac-

tivity and disapprove of others. . . .[11] (In other words primitive societies have rules and regulations concerning sex. On this point, another modern anthropologist states that anthropologists "have never found a group whose culture permitted completely unregulated relations between the sexes."[12])

(2) What is specifically approved and disapproved [about sexual behavior] may vary from one society to another.

(3) The relationship of a man and his wife is a matter of public control to the extent that the . . . group . . . has defined their rights and duties prior to the time of marriage. (This includes their sexual rights and duties.)

(4) Nowhere is divorce approved in principle, but usually some provision is made for dissolution of the union during the lifetime of the partners, for certain stated causes. (A good example of this dissolution is found in the society of the early Hebrews. Neither God nor Moses approved of divorce, but Jesus explained to the Pharisees that Moses allowed divorce because of the sinfulness of the people and because they understood so little about the real nature of love and marriage. From the beginning of creation God had created male and female so that their very nature demanded permanence in marriage—Matthew 19:3-9.)

(5) Marriage is always and everywhere legalized in a public ceremonial or religious rite.

(6) Childbirth can occur outside the family, but nowhere is illegitimacy approved. *Only within a family, within a body of recognized and accepted rules, can the duties of parents to children be regulated from one generation to the next.* Reproduction as a mere biological event is never sanctioned in human society; if it were, society could not be maintained.[13]

Radical thinkers often call our attention to such facts as: 1) the Eskimo often invites an honored guest in his home to sleep with his wife, and 2) the natives of Trobriand Island, near New Guinea, expect their children to

[11] Arnold W. Green, *Sociology, An Analysis of Life in Modern Society,* McGraw-Hill Book Company, 4th Edition, 1964, pp. 389-390.
[12] Mischa Titiev, *The Science of Man,* Henry Holt and Company, 1954, p. 367.
[13] Arnold W. Green, pp. 389-392.

have some love affairs, including sexual intercourse, before they select a permanent marriage partner. Such facts are selected and pointed out 1) to suggest that these people do not have any moral codes and 2) to suggest, therefore, that we should do away with our rules and regulations about sex. What these radical thinkers fail to point out are the facts that the Eskimos have organized family life (monogamy), have strict regulations about sex, and that if an outsider or stranger should have sexual relations with an Eskimo's wife, "He might divorce his wife, kill either wife or lover, or both, or demand restitution in economic goods."[14] Also, these radical thinkers are dishonest when they fail to point out that the natives of Trobriand Island have strict sexual rules and regulations. "Incest taboos, [sexual relations with close relatives] particularly between brother and sister, are severely enforced. It is considered highly improper for any grown or married person to mingle with the young unmarried. Lovemaking is a private affair and public displays of affection are in extreme bad taste. . . . Strangely enough . . . premarital motherhood is considered reprehensible. . . . Adultery is unmentionable in polite conversation, and is nearly unknown, and public opinion falls harshly upon the offenders."[15]

Thus, when a high school or college professor, or anyone else, argues for sexual permissiveness in our society because of a single attitude toward sex by the Eskimos or the natives of Trobriand Island, he is misleading and deceitful in his attempt to impose willfully his unsocial doctrine of unlimited sexual freedom on his students. To select an isolated part-truth (2-5 percent of the whole truth) and build the teaching of total sexual permissiveness on it when the rest of the truth involved (95-98 percent of the total truth) is in direct opposition to the small part-truth is openly dishonest. Certainly

[14] Green, p. 406.
[15] Ibid., pp. 404-405.

educated people, including high school and college professors, ought to know better.

To summarize Dr. Evelyn Duvall on the sex life of permissive societies: she points out that in a sexually permissive society, sex becomes impersonal. Appreciation for a lover, tenderness, romance, kindness, fidelity, and all of the necessary ingredients for companionship (necessary for the stable family life) tend to decline and disappear. Instead of sexual permissiveness bringing a socially perfect society, Dr. Duvall states that sexual permissiveness and family and social instability go together, since sexual permissiveness promotes major social problems such as pregnancy of single girls, abortion, venereal disease, divorce, broken families, and children who feel unloved and unwanted.[16]

Then Dr. Duvall asks youth to *"Ask yourself why the most permissive societies of the South Seas are the most underdeveloped parts of the world"* (italics added). She comments that, "Where living is easy and sex is simple, there is no reason for striving and learning and growing, either as individuals or as a culture."[17] We need to remind ourselves that in the primitive, so-called permissive societies men force themselves upon women, women have few rights, and in some places a woman is considered a "thing" or property instead of a person, and is treated accordingly. Also, in many cases, a young person is not allowed to have any part in the choice of his or her marriage companion. Often, the selection is determined by the parents through the use of astrology and superstition. We should not be allowed to forget that many of these assumed sexually permissive primitives are ignorant, in dire poverty, live in filth and squalor, are in extremely poor health, and have a low life expectancy.

Finally, Dr. Joyce O. Hertzler points out that all the ancient people who rose to a high level of organized

[16] Evelyn Millis Duvall, *Why Wait Till Marriage?*, pp. 68-69.
[17] *Ibid.*, p. 74.

Some Questions About Sex Examined

85

social and cultural civilizations (the Egyptians, Baby-lonians, Assyrians, Hittites, Persians, Hindus, Chinese, and Hebrews) had general rules and regulations that emphasized the importance of family stability, including husband-wife and parent-child relationships.[18]

Let us pray that we may come to understand that our beloved societies of the United States and the Western world must return to an emphasis on family stability, including high moral values and sexual self-control, *or* we may expect further cultural decline and decay, and must then sadly watch our high civilization quietly pass into the pages of history.

9. *Do right and wrong change from time to time and place to place?* This is another false idea held by liberal moralists who spend much of their time trying to teach youth to be sexually permissive. They believe that there is nothing permanent; *that right and wrong are determined by each society; that what is right in one society may be wrong in another and what is wrong in one society may be right in another.* Technically, sociology calls this type of thinking "cultural relativism." These advocates of permissiveness seem to be intoxicated with the idea of "social change," and they use it to encourage youth to reject past community ideas and values, and especially to encourage them to be sexually permissive before marriage. They reason with youth as follows: 1) Premarital sexual intercourse is fast increasing. Why, almost everyone is doing it, except a few narrow-minded church prudes. 2) Since everyone is doing it, it is socially acceptable and right, and, therefore, our moral codes should be changed to fall in line with what everyone is doing. As usual, they are emphasizing a small part-truth and are ignoring the rest of the truth.

We will deal with the small part-truth later. First, I would like to encourage youth to do some straight think-

[18] Joyce O. Hertzler, *Social Thought of the Ancient Civilizations,* Russell and Russell, Inc., 1961, pp. 357-359.

ing about this matter. I challenge the statement that all youth are having premarital sexual intercourse. Sociological scientific research brands this statement as *false*. Some observations about sexual scientific research are in order. First, *there has always been a great deal of premarital sex relations*. Yet, only during the last fifty years have we had any research on sexual behavior, and most of it has been during the last twenty-five years. Second, *it is difficult to secure honest factual information about a person's past sex behavior*. Many people think that this is a personal matter, and if they answer questions at all, they probably will not tell the whole truth. On the other hand, some young people will answer honestly, which may include *some who have had a premarital sexual experience only once*. They are now sorry about it, have repented of it, have been forgiven, and now insist that sex belongs to marriage. When these are asked in research, "Have you ever had sexual intercourse?" they would have to answer "Yes." Yet, these honest replies flow into the final statistical percentages and are interpreted as being in favor of premarital promiscuity. Finally, *the mass media* (television, radio, newspapers, magazines, and movies) *tend to exaggerate and place a halo on those percentages that indicate premarital sexual experience*. A liberal clergyman or college chaplain or a high school counselor can call for more sex freedom for youth, and the newspapers splash it on the front page in big headlines. On the other hand, the thousands and millions of preachers, priests, rabbis, lay leaders, and other moral people who believe sex belongs to marriage are ignored. Their ideas are not newsworthy. Little wonder many are so confused about the place of sex during the period from puberty to marriage.

In spite of these rather gloomy comments about sexual scientific research, I insist that trained, skillful, honest sociologists can and should gather scientific facts about sexual behavior in our society. We have done so and will continue to do so. Such sociologists, including Ernest

W. Burgess, Paul Wallin, Evelyn Millis Duvall, Clark Vincent, Robert O. Blood, Harold T. Christensen, Judson and Mary Landis, Winston W. Ehrmann, and Paul Popenoe, to name only a few, have done rather accurate research on premarital sex relations. These sociologists —and others including psychologists and biologists— have used scientific research to help us understand, positively, the relation of sexual behavior to health, individual personality development, morals, husband-wife relationships, family happiness, and community stability. Negatively, they have used scientific research to measure the relationship of the misuse and abuse of sex to venereal diseases, mental and emotional disturbances, social delinquency, vice, and crime. When all this that is related to the rate of premarital sex is summarized, I can agree with Dr. Evelyn Duvall who says that in the United States, "The best educated guess [from the research] is that perhaps half the men and one-fourth of the women college students have had coital experience by the time they reach twenty-one."[19] Thus we can state categorically that the assumption that "everyone is doing it" is simply not true. Those who are "doing it" are in the minority. Thus the radical thinkers' first argument is only a part-truth.

But let us look further at the characteristics of this minority in the light of scientific research. Judson and Mary Landis state that:

> Certain types of personality weaknesses or maladjustment may contribute to excessive sexual emphasis before marriage, and these same factors may contribute to failure in marriage. Research studies have shown a combination of background factors to be related to marriage failure. Among people whose marriages end in divorce there are more who
> (1) are from unhappy or divorced homes;
> (2) had no close relationship with parents;
> (3) were from families with no religious affiliation or with antagonistic attitudes toward religion;

[19] Duvall, p. 15.

Sexual Understanding Before Marriage

(4) have, themselves, no religious affiliation or are antagonistic toward religion.

In all our research studies these same factors were found to be significantly associated with non-virginity in college students, both men and women[20] (numbers and italics added).

These personality weaknesses and maladjustments associated with sexual permissiveness are largely played down or ignored by the mass media and the sex promoters.

The question that must be faced by Christian youth and all who want a stable society is not the prevalence or non-prevalence of premarital sex relations, although this information is important. The question before us is *what is right and what is wrong?* Most of us will agree that right and wrong are not determined either by the minority or the majority behavior in any society. Right and wrong are inherent in, are anchored in, and are determined by the plan of the Creator as He planned and created the world of nature and created male and female in His image and placed them in the midst of the natural creation. Those who say it is impossible to know what is right and what is wrong are simply avoiding the issue and often simply do not want to know. We can determine right and wrong through a combination of sources: 1) divine revelation, 2) scientific research, 3) personal experience, 4) historical experience, and 5) reason.

We are not only concerned about right and wrong, but Christian youth and all responsible people are also concerned about such significant questions as:

(1) What kind of behavior will develop normal personalities in childhood?

(2) What kind of behavior will develop responsible youth?

(3) What kind of behavior will develop mature adults?

[20] Landis, 5th Edition, p. 133.

(4) What kind of behavior will develop stable family life?

(5) What kind of behavior will develop efficient social institutions?

(6) What kind of behavior will develop effective government?

(7) What kind of behavior will develop a high civilization?

Any youth who is not interested in the right answers to these questions has simply stopped thinking and certainly does not have a bright future.

We are now ready to examine the second part of the argument of the radical thinkers which contends that, "since everyone is doing it (which we have shown to be false), premarital sex relations are socially acceptable and right, and therefore all our moral codes should be changed to fall in line with what everyone is doing." These "thinkers" continually stress the importance of "social change" to high school and college students. In this argument through skillful intellectual trickery they trap honest young people into believing deceptive ideas. The terms "social change and progress" appeal to youth; they appeal to most of us. Much social change is good. But to trick youth into accepting loose morals and premarital permissiveness, their reasoning follows certain deceptive patterns. For example, they point out the change and progress we have made in our places of habitation. Primitive people lived in caves, and later in mud huts. Then came log cabins, frame houses, brick houses, stone mansions, and finally the houses we have today. Then follows a second example, progress in modes of travel. Our progress includes changing from walking, to ox carts, to wagons, to buggies, to surries, to automobiles, to airplanes, and now to rockets. Of course, all this is true. At this point, without warning youth, they spring their trap. They continue the argument by saying that it used to be that people had strict moral rules about sex outside of marriage. But we live in a society of social change, and we are constantly making social progress. Gradually our society has changed until almost all young people are having premarital sex relations. In only a few years it will be one hundred percent. Therefore, since everyone is doing it, it is high time that we change all our moral codes to correspond with our progressive culture.

The trap, the dishonesty of this reasoning, is obvious to thinking young people. They fail to warn you that the reasoning shifts from things (houses and modes of travel) to persons (premarital sex relations); that the reasoning shifts from physical, inanimate objects to human behavior on the mental, emotional, spiritual, moral, and social levels. They fail to warn that the increasing knowledge of mankind about the world of nature and its applications to society is always changing, but that basically the nature and needs of human beings have changed very little, if at all, across the centuries. In commenting on this type of dishonest thinking, Judson and Mary Landis quote Walter Waggoner as saying that we need to be careful not to "confuse the ailment with the desired state of health, or change the temperature scales on the thermometer to make the fever normal."[21]

Following through on Waggoner's comment, let us note how ridiculous the above argument involving social change is by observing two illustrations. Imagine that ninety percent of the people in the state of Indiana have developed ulcers. Would it be logical for the Medical Association of Indiana to rewrite their medical books stating that it is healthy for people to develop ulcers because "everybody is doing it," and to suggest ten good ways to develop ulcers? Or, suppose that during a fever epidemic in the state of Tennessee, ninety percent of the citizens develop a fever of 103°. Would the Tennessee Medical Association have the factories that make thermometers change the normal fever mark on all the

[21] Landis, 2nd Edition, p. 133.

thermometers from 98° plus to 103°? What stupid questions! Yet this is the same type of reasoning these people have been using to promote sexual permissiveness. They are saying "since everyone is doing it, we must change all moral rules and regulations to follow what everyone is doing." Rubbish! This is purely academic nonsense and intellectual ignorance. It is barnyard thinking. It would lead civilization straight back to the jungle; and these thinkers are educated people—people who ought to know better. They are certainly lacking in judgment and wisdom. We would hope that thinking people are too smart to be caught in this obvious trap.

Finally, let us examine the fact—the part-truth—that we referred to earlier: social change does and should affect our accepted behavior patterns to some degree. It is only a part-truth to say that Christians have always resisted social change. And while it is true that many older people do resist social change, many kinds of people with *many* different philosophies resist social change. I can remember when I refused to wear a wrist watch because I thought it was sissy. I can also remember when I made fun of friends for playing golf; I called it "cow pasture pool." (I have been playing golf now for thirty years!) Christians have adjusted to and followed social change in our society across the years. They have moved from log cabins to efficient houses. Most have changed from the horse and buggy to the automobile and to the airplane. They use the electric refrigerator and the air conditioner. They use radio and television for Christian witnessing. And some of the astronauts have been mature Christians.

However, the degree with which we follow social change, the mores, folkways, and simple habits of people about us has to be limited by the broad basic principles of Christianity as revealed in Scripture. In general, evangelical Christians believe that Christians should follow social change in our society so long as it does not violate:

(1) the teachings and principles taught in the Scriptures, including the Ten Commandments and the moral laws of God,
(2) known scientific facts,
(3) personality development toward maturity,
(4) our physical, mental, and emotional health,
(5) our own personal needs and rights, and
(6) the personal needs and rights of other persons.

The culture of any society must change within the framework of the total will and purpose of God and His plan for the world of nature, including the interpersonal and sexual relationships between men and women, or it will gradually erode, decline, and decay.

10. *Does the New Morality make our past sex traditions out of date?* Many honest and·sincere young people seem to think so. It is not easy to give a simple, yet accurate, reply to this question so that youth may understand it thoroughly. The reason for this difficulty is that the so-called New Morality is a complex mixture of philosophy, theology, and ethics advocated by a few intellectuals who follow the extreme in current liberal secular theology. The problem is made more difficult since, as usual, the false theory of the New Morality contains some important *part-truths* that are part of the central core of Christianity. We will attempt to translate the theory of the New Morality into simple language and point out its strengths and its weaknesses so that the average high school student can understand it and the problems involved.[22]

[22] This interpretation of the New Morality is based upon the following sources: (1) Joseph Fletcher, *Situation Ethics* (The Westminster Press, 1966); (2) Harvey Cox, Editor, *The Situation Ethics Debate* (The Westminster Press, 1968), especially the article by Henlee H. Barnette, pp. 121-146; (3) Arthur F. Holmes, Review of Joseph Fletcher's *Situation Ethics* in *Christianity Today,* June 23, 1967, p. 30; (4) Merville O. Vincent, Review of Harvey Cox's *The Situation Ethics Debate* in *Christianity Today,* July 19, 1968, p. 38; (5) "God's Will for a Wayward Age," editorial in *Christianity Today,* December 22, 1967, pp. 24-26; (6) T. B. Maston, "The New Morality," *Baptist and Reflector,* November, 1968, p. 12; and (7) Paul Popenoe, "The Permissive Morality," *Family Life,* June, 1966, pp. 1-4.

The strong points and the part-truths of the New Morality can be summarized in five basic principles.

(1) It emphasizes the *importance of love.*

(2) It emphasizes the *importance and the rights of all individual persons.*

(3) It emphasizes the *freedom of individual persons.*

(4) It seems to say that *educated mature youth will make right decisions,* and should be trusted to do so, including all decisions about sex.

(5) It emphasizes the fact that there are *some social situations in our lives in which it is difficult to decide what is right and what is wrong.*

These five basic principles sound good. They ring true; they appeal to thinking people, both young and old. But it is necessary for us to examine these principles in light of the *total teachings of the New Morality advocates* and in light of the *total teachings of the Bible.*

Let us now describe the weak points of the New Morality.

(1) The New Morality's definition of love is not the Bible definition of love. The Bible teaches us that "God is love," that love is the very nature of God, that the supreme expression of love was God's love for us when He sent Christ to the cross to die for us, and that Christian behavior ought to be characterized by the kind of love God has for us in Christ. On the other hand, the New Morality seems to make love a *human* something. It seems to make human love by and in itself the absolute authority in deciding what is right and what is wrong. We all know that there are many levels of love—such as, 1) God's love for mankind, 2) a man's love for his wife, 3) a person's love for parents, brothers, and sisters, 4) a youth's love for a sweetheart, 5) a person's love for food, and 6) a boy's love for his dog. Likewise, we all know that there are few words that are more misused, abused, and misunderstood than the word love. Advocates of the New Morality are chief among sinners

in their shifting of meanings, misusing and abusing the word love.

(2) The New Morality's emphasis on the rights and freedom of persons is carried to a false extreme. They seem to be saying that the source of all authority rests within the individual himself, and his love determines what is right and what is wrong. This is in direct conflict with the teachings of the Bible. For example, Jesus said, "All power is given unto me in heaven and in earth" (Matthew 28:18). Jesus is called "King of Kings, and Lord of Lords" (Revelation 19:16). Paul said, "Whatsoever ye do in word or deed, do all in the name of the Lord Jesus" (Colossians 3:17). This last passage literally is saying that a Christian ought to make all the decisions concerning his life and behavior in accord with the teachings and will of Christ our Savior. *The Christian approach to right and wrong is that ultimate and final authority resides in God our Creator who revealed Himself to us in Christ.* Christians are to seek the will of God in their lives. The individual is important and does have freedom of choice, but by nature the Christian *wants to choose to follow the will of God* in deciding what is right and what is wrong.

(3) The New Morality emphasizes the importance of "inner motives" and plays down the importance of overt external acts. Actually, the advocates of the New Morality are as much out of line with the teachings of Jesus as were the Pharisees of Jesus' day. They are the Pharisees of today—in reverse. The Pharisees ignored inner motives and emphasized the importance of external acts. They used their own man-made rules to determine which acts were right and which were wrong. The will of God and divine principles were ignored. Following these rules, they would not work on the Sabbath, but would decide to kill a man on the Sabbath. Today, the New Morality tends to ignore the importance of external acts and emphasizes the significance of inner motives. But, like the Pharisees, the rightness or wrongness of an inner

motive is determined by humanistic man-made rules. The act is good because the individual thinks it is good. Thus, premarital sexual intercourse is good if the two individuals involved think it is good. The will of God and divine principles are ignored.

A wise and sensitive youth must protest this unwarranted emphasis on the absolute authority of the individual. Historic Christianity has never separated inner motives and external acts and treated them as if they were unrelated. Rather, Christianity has defended the concept that our inner motives and our external acts are both a part of us. One is as real as the other. They are simply opposite aspects of the same person. Jesus, in His emphasis on inner motives, was trying to correct the false ideas of the Pharisees. He did not intend to teach that external acts are insignificant as the New Morality implies.

(4) The New Morality seems to be saying that educated mature youth (or adults) will make right decisions. This assumes that human nature is good. It avoids and ignores the real nature of human beings which tends to be sinful, proud, vain, egotistical, selfish, self-centered, and irrational. It ignores what theology calls the "depth of human depravity." What does the Bible have to say on this subject? The writer of Ecclesiastes said, "There is not a just man upon earth, that doeth good, and sinneth not" (Ecclesiastes 7:20). Isaiah says, "All we like sheep have gone astray; we have turned every one to his own way; and the Lord hath laid on him the iniquity of us all" (Isaiah 53:6). Jesus said, "Ye are of your father the devil, and the lusts of your father will ye do" (John 8:44). Paul said, "For all have sinned, and come short of the glory of God" (Romans 3:23). There are many other similar passages, including John 8:7; Romans 7:14-25; I Corinthians 15:22.

(5) The New Morality overemphasizes the fact that in social situations it is difficult to decide what is right and what is wrong. It seems to be saying that in all human

decisions in all social situations it is difficult to decide between right and wrong. The New Morality says there are no universal laws that bind us in all of our decisions of conduct. This makes the Ten Commandments out of date. It makes love a "codeless" love; that is, since we must follow our own human love, we must reject all law, including the Ten Commandments. According to the New Morality there is no black or white, but *all* human choices and decisions are shades of gray. For the Christian this idea must be rejected as an excessive exaggeration of a small part-truth.

It is true that there are some social situations in which it is difficult to decide what is right and what is wrong. These decisions may rightfully be referred to as "gray" decisions. However, the cold fact is that Christians who want to follow the will of God have no trouble deciding on right and wrong in most social situations. They know that it is wrong to lie, to cheat, to steal, to commit fornication or adultery. In my judgment, approximately ninety or ninety-five percent or more of life's decisions are either right or wrong. The philosophy of the New Morality seems to be saying through the mass media that "It is a sin to be good" and "It is good to do evil." The Bible warns us against this kind of thinking when it says, "Woe unto them that call evil good, and good evil; that put darkness for light, and light for darkness; that put bitter for sweet, and sweet for bitter!" (Isaiah 5:20).

Since it is true that there are some isolated social situations that seem to justify violating one of the Ten Commandments, let us examine an imaginary case. Often complex ideas can be reduced to simple truths by the use of apt illustrations.

Suppose a pilot is forced to land his airplane at sea. The plane sinks, but he manages to salvage and inflate his rubber life raft. He drifts for a few days without food. Finally he sights land and maneuvers his raft to shore. Once ashore he discovers a hut which is serving as headquarters for a team of surveyors who are away on this specific day on a surveying expedition. The hungry man breaks open the door, goes in, discovers food, and eats some of it. Technically, he has stolen property that belongs to someone else. Yet, if he were brought before the legal courts, he would not be convicted of this as a crime, because the extreme circumstances of this situation dictate that it was right for him to eat the food. After eating, the exhausted man uses the two-way radio system in the hut to notify the outside world that he is safe. The surveyors, picking up the message, rush back to the hut and greet the man, not as a thief, but as a hero and a friend. This is a social situation in which the circumstances and motives involved made it right to steal. The following observations are in order:

(a) This is a rare isolated social situaiton.

(b) The motive for taking the food was good—survival of a person in a situation over which he had no control.

(c) The results of the acts were good—the man survived.

(d) The fact that it was right for the pilot to steal in this situation did not repeal the eighth commandment: "Thou shalt not steal" (Exodus 20:15).

(e) It is easy for selfish, sinful human beings to rationalize and classify their situation as rare and isolated to attempt a justification for committing almost any sin, including permissive sexual sins.

(f) It is easy for the liberal New Morality to assume that there are more of these isolated cases than there really are. The "gray" between the black and white is not nearly as extensive as we have been led to believe by some.

Secondly, let us examine an actual experience told by Joseph Fletcher in which he illustrates the ideas of the New Morality as they are related to committing adultery.

During World War II, a German woman, a Mrs. Bergmeier, while fleeing from the advancing Russian army, was captured by the Russians and sent to a concentration camp in the Ukraine. Her children escaped; her husband, a German soldier, had been captured in the Battle of the Bulge and was in a British military prison camp. When her husband was released from prison after the war, he finally located their three children, ages, ten, twelve, and fifteen, and settled down in Germany in dire financial need and greatly in need of the mother. Their efforts to locate her failed. Finally, information reached Mrs. Bergmeier that her family was together and searching for her. The Russian rules were that no woman could be released from the prison camp unless she was extremely ill or pregnant. In case of illness, she would be sent to a Russian hospital; in case of pregnancy, she would be sent back to Germany. In this predicament, Dr. Fletcher says:

> She turned things over in her mind and finally asked a friendly Volga German camp guard to impregnate her, which he did. Her condition being medically verified, she was sent back to Berlin and to her family. They welcomed her with open arms, even when she told them how she had managed it. When the child was born, they loved him more than all the rest, on the view that little Dietrich had done more for them than anybody.[23]

The following observations are in order concerning this illustration:

(a) It was a rare isolated social situation.
(b) Mrs. Bergmeier's sole motive was not lust, but rather to be released from the prison camp, to survive, and to be reunited with her family. This motive was socially good.
(c) The results of the act were socially good. She was in a situation for which she was not responsible and over which she had no control. As a result of the act, she survived, was released, and was happily reunited with her family.

Was her decision "right or wrong"? It is in order to

[23] Joseph Fletcher, *Situation Ethics: The New Morality,* The Westminster Press, 1966, pp. 164-165.

point out that there have been many Christians in the past and there are many now living who would rather languish in prison than to violate one of God's commandments. However, for the purpose of further reasoning, let us assume that Mrs. Bergmeier's act was right. Assuming her act was right, what effect would this assumption have on the seventh commandment, "Thou shalt not commit adultery"? It would not change it, repeal it, or have any effect on it at all. It would still stand as a permanent command from God that it is wrong and sinful to commit adultery.

Since Mr. and Mrs. Bergmeier were Christians, they would probably be among the first to admit that adultery is evil.

We live in an evil world, and that world sometimes forces upon us choices that have no clear "right" solution. We are sometimes forced to the lesser of two evils, but that does not make the lesser evil good. What Mrs. Bergmeier did was wrong.

Let us repeat, it is easy for the New Morality to encourage selfish, sinful human beings to rationalize and classify their particular social situation as being a rare and an isolated case which justifies their committing any sin, including permissive sexual sins. It is easy for them to assume falsely that all of their social situations are gray, and that there is really no black or white. This is especially true since the New Morality rejects all universal moral laws and anchors the source of all authority about right and wrong with the individual person and his or her interpretation of "love." It is easy for insecure, untrained youth to shift the Biblical meaning of love to a human level and identify it with sexual attraction. Imagine a sophisticated high school couple, who have a vague acquaintance with the New Morality teachings, in the back seat of a parked car! How would the New Morality teachings affect them? Or how would the New Morality teachings affect an engaged couple, age twenty-one, in similar circumstances? Obviously, these youth would say, "We are mature; we love each other. Why not?"

Christian youth must not be afraid of these part-truths at the center of the original New Morality teachings, but these must be understood in the light of the total moral truth taught by Christianity and society across the years.

Arthur F. Holmes states the case against the New Morality in accurate language when he says that it "fails to see that the Biblical alternative to legalism (law without love or liberty) is not situationism (love and liberty without law) but a Biblical personalism that unites love with law as well as liberty, giving content to love and guaranteeing liberty."[24]

[24] Holmes, Review, *Situation Ethics,* p. 30.

CHAPTER 7

OTHER PERTINENT QUESTIONS ABOUT
SEX DISCUSSED

This then is the message which we have heard of him, and declare unto you, that God is light, and in him is no darkness at all. If we say that we have fellowship with him, and walk in darkness, we lie, and do not the truth: But if we walk in the light, as he is in the light, we have fellowship one with another, and the blood of Jesus Christ his Son cleanseth us from all sin. If we say that we have no sin, we deceive ourselves, and the truth is not in us. If we confess our sins, he is faithful and just to forgive us our sins, and to cleanse us from all unrighteousness. *(I John 1:5-9, KJV)*

You young people have a way of asking questions which are serious, honest, and which strike at the heart of reality. But this is nothing new. Youth has always asked questions and will continue to do so in years to come. This questioning and receiving of thorough, frank, and objective answers is actually the heart of the learning process. Today, many young people are being encouraged by radical "self-appointed intellectuals" to ask questions designed to destroy Christian morality. And yet, the majority of these questions have grown out of youth's own honest personal struggles toward maturity. Let us focus our attention upon ten such questions and discuss them.

1. *Why is sexual intercourse evil before marriage and good after marriage?* When this question is asked, I get

the feeling that the one asking it is assuming, probably without realizing it, that Christianity teaches that sex is evil. He really does not think about the One who created it. Of course, to assume that sex is evil is false; nothing that God created is evil. It is only the human misuse and abuse of sex that is wrong.

All of us, young and old, are in the stream of God's creation. Our lives follow an unfolding process that slowly develops from birth to mature adulthood. We can do very little to hurry the physical, mental, emotional, and spiritual processes that carry us to maturity. A twelve-year-old boy cannot play on a professional basketball team, nor can he be a jet pilot. Why? Because the structure of the stream of God's created order involves some limitation in early life.

To give a small child a razor might bring him happiness, but the dangers involved are too great to run such a risk. So it is with sexual experimentation before marriage. The risks are just not worth the momentary pleasure. The time will arrive when the individual will be mature enough to leave his parents and in marriage cleave to the one he loves and then to experience the joys that come with this unity. Marriage is for adults—mature adults who are able to cope with the responsibilities of marriage. These responsibilities involve economic stability, meeting emotional needs of another person, parenthood, and community life.

You might ask: "What about premarital sex for single people who are older and mature? I know that it is quite fashionable today, especially, for single men and women who are in the working world to entertain the opposite sex overnight in their apartments." Yes, they're single; they're older. Yes, they're mature physically, but mentally and emotionally—no! For a person to give of himself sexually out of the bonds of wedlock can only lead him to despair, and, in time, will leave him as void and empty as a room without furnishings. Sex is not like taking a glass of water when one is thirsty. Too much emotional rapture and giving of oneself occur during and after the sex act. In all my years of counseling, I have found this to be true—premarital sex *just won't work!* It only leads to tears and heartaches!

2. *What is the difference between an engaged couple three months to three weeks before marriage and the same couple after marriage?* Some seem to assume that there is really no difference between a couple a few weeks before marriage and the same couple a few weeks after marriage. To show that this assumption is in error, let us examine five major and significant differences between these two states.[1]

(1) Before marriage a couple is involved in and dependent on two separate economic systems. The boy and girl are each a part of their respective family units. Their parents are responsible to them for food, clothing, shelter, and protection. After marriage, however, the couple is a separate economic unit, and the two together are now responsible for their own food, clothing, shelter, protection, and other needs.

(2) Before marriage the boy and girl have been conditioned by approximately two decades of psychological, emotional, social, and spiritual experience with their own families. Most of their teachings, beliefs, values, and ways of life have now become a real part of their inner self. Of course, after marriage they still will love their parents and will cherish the values and relationships received from them; but then they must depend upon each other for inner strength, stability, and support.

(3) Before marriage both the boy and girl are identified legally with their own individual parents. They are two separate legal entities who are free to act within the framework of his or her own family according to the laws of his or her particular state. After marriage, these two legal entities are merged into one unit. They are

[1] Adapted from "Moralism and Sex Ethics: A Defense," by William Hamilton, *Christianity and Crisis: A Christian Journal of Opinion,* October 28, 1957, Volume XVII, No. 18, p. 142.

legally bound to each other and are legally responsible to each other. Although they are still the son and daughter of their own parents, their legal status has been changed to that of a family unit.

(4) Before marriage they are not one in the eyes of the social community. Their relatives, friends, and community associates see them as members of their own families and expect them to perform the social and moral roles of single people. After marriage their relatives and friends see them as members of a new family unit and expect them to perform the social and moral roles of married people.

(5) Before marriage, if a pregnancy should occur, there is immediately before them a mountain of personal, emotional, social, and spiritual problems that would tend to be a major burden to them the rest of their lives. After marriage, if and when a pregnancy occurs, the baby would be accepted, loved, and cared for as an equal member of the new family unit and of the community.

The assumption that there is no difference between a couple three weeks or three months before marriage and the same couple three weeks or three months after marriage is simply not in accord with the real facts involved. There are differences—important ones!

It may be that a clear definition of Christian marriage will help us to see, in proper perspective, the differences in the before and the after states of marriage.

Dr. Derrick Bailey in his excellent volume, *The Mystery of Love and Marriage,* states that a Christian marriage is completed when the following takes place: (a) the boy and girl love each other; (b) each acts freely, deliberately, rationally, and responsibly; (c) each acts in the knowledge and approval of the community; (d) they act in conformity with divine law; and (e) they unite their lives through sexual intercourse.[2]

[2] Derrick Sherwin Bailey, *The Mystery of Love and Marriage,* Harper and Row, 1952, p. 52.

In the light of this definition of Christian marriage, it is immediately obvious that couples who are in love and engaged and have sexual intercourse before marriage have violated Christian marriage in three specific ways:

(1) They have acted secretly without the knowledge or approval of the social community. There has been no legal license, no public announcement, and no public or private marriage ceremony.

(2) They have violated divine law and divine will.

(3) Their decision was not made rationally or responsibly. Rather it was made in the heat of sexual passion, and they risked the possibility of children being born out of wedlock.

Let us imagine that a couple is in love, engaged, purchases a marriage license, has a public wedding ceremony, and moves into their own house. Although they are capable of doing so, let us suppose that *they never have sexual intercourse.* Would this constitute a legal Christian marriage? A careful study of the Scriptures and due consideration of all the factors involved make it necessary to conclude that it would not. There have been such cases where couples have lived for five or ten years in this type of marriage, and the marriage was finally annulled on the grounds that it had never been consummated. Therefore, divorce was not necessary.

We must hasten to say that a Christian marriage is much more than just having sexual intercourse. On the other hand, in the plan of the Creator, marriage is a sexual relationship also. This relationship is one of His finest gifts to man and woman. Thus, sexual intercourse before marriage is evil; it is fornication and must be rejected. Sex belongs to marriage. It is inherent in the very nature of Christian marriage.

3. *Does sexual self-control before marriage cause dangerous psychological repressions that will destroy normal sex life and personality in marriage?* Judson and Mary Landis point out that certain people often argue that youth must either: (1) marry at early ages, (2) have

sex expression through promiscuity or premarital relationships, or (3) inhibit their natural urges to the point of dangerous self-repression.[3]

The following is a summary of the Landises' reply to these charges: Several fallacies exist in such reasoning. The first one is the assumption that marriage is only legal sexual indulgence. The second fallacy is the assumption that the alternative is either premarital indulgence or dangerous repression. This ignores the possibility of self-control. The third fallacy argues that control of sex impulses before marriage leads to overrepression that may handicap later marital adjustment. Repressions that are dangerous are not developed in young adulthood, but rather they are developed in early childhood and are due to the faults in our system of sex education.[4]

It is not only necessary to agree with the Landises, but to say that, contrary to the thinking of some secular materialistic intellectuals, there is no scientific evidence that premarital self-control is detrimental to normal emotional life or a hazard to successful marriage.

4. *Why is it necessary to have rules and regulations?* Often teen-agers rebel against the rules of their parents and the laws of society and honestly, yet impatiently, ask, "Why is it necessary for us to have rules and regulations? Why can't we be free to do what we want to do?" Let us discuss this question of rules and regulations. It is true that the different nations of the world have a variety of social and moral customs and patterns of behavior. For example, the values and customs of the United States are different than those of India. We consider some Indian customs absurd, as they, in turn, consider some of ours. But it does not follow from this that there should be no rules and regulations in life. Let us illustrate the facts involved.

Mathematics follows many rules. Two plus two always equals four, and the square of the hypotenuse always

---

[3] Landis, *Building a Successful Marriage,* 4th Edition, p. 187.
[4] *Ibid.,* pp. 187-188.

equals the sum of the squares of the other two sides of a right triangle. In physics the two major rules are: (1) Energy can change its form (from solid, to liquid, to gas) but not its quantity. (2) There is a universal tendency in the universe for disorder and decay. Chemistry follows many rules, such as: Two parts of hydrogen and one part of oxygen always equal water. Water, in our atmosphere, always boils at 212 degrees Fahrenheit and always freezes at 32 degrees Fahrenheit.

When the pilot of a plane is forced to land his plane in darkness and heavy clouds by instructions from the airport tower, he follows rigidly the rules and regulaitons given by the radar tower operator. When a jet plane lands by instruments, the plane instruments follow mechanically the rules and regulations flashed from the ground instruments.

When the astronauts fly by rocket to the moon, both the ground crew and the astronauts follow precisely and meticulously the rules and regulations of the earth's atmosphere and the pull of gravity of both the earth and the moon. These are the rules that God set up in creation for our solar system.

In recreational and professional sports, such as baseball, basketball, and football, there is always a book of rules and regulations that each side must follow.

In the area of the health of the physical body there are many rules and regulations. We human beings must eat food and drink water, or we will die. There are no exceptions to this rule. To be healthy we must follow the rules and regulations of scientific nutrition.

In the mental and emotional realms, a person must follow rules and regulations to become normal and mature. Any person who is self-centered, who increasingly develops fear of other people, distrust of himself, and lives in isolated anxiety will sooner or later be confined to a mental institution or the grave. On the other hand, a person who gets his mind off himself, who has altruistic objectives outside of himself, and who is determined to help and to serve other people, will develop a healthy self-confidence and will live a happy, balanced normal life. Jesus stated these psychological rules when He said, "Whosoever shall exalt himself shall be abased; and he that shall humble himself shall be exalted" (Matthew 23:12).

Dr. Arnold Green, in discussing the subject of right and wrong as related to society, says: "Human society is built upon this web of should and ought. Without moral norms (rules), human society would perish...."[5]

It is surprising and somewhat amusing that some people seem to think that only Christians advocate rules and regulations. All schools of thought, all social groups, and all individuals have rules. Even those who emphasize materialistic ideas and oppose Christian ideas are governed by their own little regulatory system. Some examples of their rules are: (1) Thou shalt emphasize the physical as the ultimate in life. (2) Thou shalt not believe in God or anything that is non-physical. (3) Thou shalt follow thine own individual desires and impulses. (4) Thou shalt not submit to group or social limitations.

Sociologist Arnold Green aptly comments: "Even those groups who flagrantly violate the common moral norms must preserve their own specialized moral norms; members of a criminal gang should not 'squeal' on their associates."[6] Thus, even criminal gangs rigidly follow rules and regulations.

These few examples illustrate the fact that the universe in which we live is a unity of friendly, interlocking, cooperating laws. God created it thus. Wherever we turn in life we are confronted by these laws: rules and regulations. They are real. We follow them largely without question. When we do not follow them, we suffer disastrous consequences. As we violate laws, we either gradually or quickly destroy ourselves, depending on the

[5] Arnold W. Green, *Sociology, An Analysis of Life in Modern Society*, p. 39.
[6] *Ibid.*, p. 39.

laws violated. One may steal for a long time and get by with it, but when a person jumps off the top of a twenty-story skyscraper, he violates the law of gravity only once. But sooner or later the thief will be caught and will pay the penalty for his violations. It is not difficult for thinking people to understand and accept the reasoning that if there are rules and regulations that must be followed in the realms of the physical, mental, and emotional, then there will have to be some social, moral, and spiritual laws to regulate the interpersonal relationships between a person and any other person or group of persons. Thus we have laws against stealing, adultery, and murder. A community without laws would degenerate into anarchy, into a "dog-eat-dog" jungle.

Since God created man and woman in His image, we are free persons, within limits. This freedom is one of mankind's greatest blessings. God expects us to be responsible in exercising our freedom. There is really no conflict between following laws and being free to choose. The more we obey the laws (natural, moral, and divine), the greater our freedom becomes. The more we violate laws, the less freedom we have, and the more we become slaves to these violations. A person is free to drink whiskey, but the more whiskey a person drinks, the sooner he becomes an alcoholic—a slave to alcohol. A person is free to be sexually promiscuous, but the more promiscuous he becomes, the sooner he contracts venereal disease and destroys his health, his family, and his social life. When a youth exercises his freedom to control sex until marriage, he has followed the moral and spiritual laws of the Bible and society. In marriage he will have the freedom to enjoy happy sexual experiences regularly. In marriage this free sexual happiness does not destroy but develops continued maturity and self-fulfillment.

When youth asks, "Why do we have to follow rules and regulations?" thoughtful parents, teachers, and other counselors answer that laws are inherent in the nature of our world and in the nature of our own lives. It is impossible to avoid or escape from the realities of our own nature. It is easy for some to become anxiously concerned and extremely rebellious over one or two rules, such as not drinking alcoholic beverages or controlling sex until marriage, and to ignore dozens and dozens of free choices open to them.

Let us learn a lesson from a baby. At birth a baby is extremely selfish and self-centered. He has had no social experience. His parents must protect him by forcing him to follow certain rules and regulations. They must see that he has food to eat, is kept in proper room temperature, and is kept from falling or from touching a hot stove. If the parents did not do this, the baby would not survive. As the baby grows older, the parents work hard to teach their child to follow the necessary rules and regulations in order that he may survive and use the freedom God meant for all of us to enjoy. Let us remember that (1) the laws of the universe and most laws of our society really give us freedom, (2) these laws are our real friends and not our enemies, and (3) human life would not be meaningful apart from the rules and regulations inherent in the plan of creation.

5. *How can youth know where to draw the line between right and wrong?* Actually the process of determining what is right and what is wrong is not nearly as difficult and complicated as some people have tried to lead us to believe. It seems rather obvious that some people do not want to know what is right or wrong and, in self-defense, keep asking, "How can we know?"

One gets the feeling that those who are continually saying or implying that it is impossible to distinguish between right and wrong are really displaying a defensive smoke screen to hide their own questionable ideas, and possibly their own violation of accepted and necessary moral laws.

What is the proper approach to finding out what is right and what is wrong? I suggest five approaches.

(1) Revelation: The Bible is the record of God's revelation of Himself to mankind in the person of Jesus Christ, and is concerned about such things as sin, salvation, a Christian social order, and eternal life. It is not a specialized book of ethics, nor does it give minute details about the rightness and wrongness of every possible act or behavior. However, it does set forth broad basic principles that can be applied to any isolated situation. The Bible is not lacking in information to help a person shun wrong and get on the side of right.

2) Science: During the last hundred years the use of the scientific method in such areas as physics, chemistry, biology, psychology, sociology, and anthropology has discovered many facts about the nature of human life that are exceedingly helpful in determining what is right and what is wrong. This is specific knowledge that is not found in the Scriptures and yet is not in conflict with the truths that are stated therein. This scientific information supplements the Bible. For example, thanks to science, we now know that smoking cigarettes can cause lung cancer, heart disease, strokes, and emphysema. Thus, we know definitely that smoking cigarettes is harmful, yet, we did not learn this directly from the Bible.

(3) Historical experience: The pages of history are filled with the experiences of many religious, social, political, and national groups who have wrestled with the moral problems involved in human behavior and progress. Many times in history our forefathers have profited by the mistakes and the right decisions of their predecessors. Any person or group can receive much help about what is right and wrong by a thorough study of the events occurring in past history.

(4) Personal experience: Often little children do not believe there is anything wrong with touching a hot stove until they put their hand on one. Many people with closed minds have argued that there is nothing wrong with a certain pattern of behavior, only to learn

otherwise through a personal encounter with that behavior. Personal experience is a great teacher.

(5) Reason: God is a rational, reasonable Person who wants His children to be reasonable. In determining right from wrong in any situation a Christian can study Bible principles and the known scientific facts related to the problem and can then reason logically about the act or behavior under consideration. Although reason has its limitations, it is an excellent tool to use in an honest attempt to determine the rightness or wrongness of any act or social situation.

Often young people individually or in discussion groups have asked me to draw an exact line between sexual right and wrong before marriage. This I have always refused to do. It is not my responsibility to make individual decisions for youth. However, it is my responsibility, and it is the responsibility of our homes, churches, schools, and communities, to help youth think through the total reality involved in drawing the line between sexual right and wrong. Unfortunately, my generation has failed miserably in giving youth the help they have wanted and needed. The radical thinkers have kept repeating and shouting to our youth such small part-truths and absurd lies as, "It is impossible to draw the line between right and wrong"; "The decisions are left entirely up to the individuals involved"; "Right and wrong change from time to time and place to place"; and "Scientific progress has outdated our puritanical, traditional moral rules." We may be certain that these wild ideas did not come from the Holy Scriptures. Also, in light of these preachments it is easy to understand why some are confused about sex before marriage. Young people need help in drawing the line, and most want help.

In previous chapters we have attempted to outline a framework of ideas about premarital sexual realities to assist youth in decision making. At this point, the outline may be summarized as follows:

(1) Petting, and "making out" on casual dates, is wrong.

(2) When a mature couple feels certain they love each other or are in a sincere engagement, a *limited* pattern of affection at the proper time, the proper place, with the proper understanding and the proper restraint involving bodily contact is normal and within the framework of Christian ideals.

(3) Sexual intercourse belongs to marriage.

(4) *Unlimited* sexual arousal belongs to marriage. It is the plan of God for husbands and wives in marriage to prepare for sexual intercourse.

(5) Sexual orgasms belong to marriage. They are the end-result of unlimited sexual arousal and/or sexual intercourse.

These five propositions have been thoroughly tested and substantiated by the Scriptures, by scientific research, by historical and personal experience, and by reason. Therefore, they are responsible guidelines that youth may trust in making their own decisions as to the right time, the right place, the right understanding, and the right restraint. Although these guidelines are broad, they give youth the freedom to decide how and where their own pattern of affection involving bodily contact shall be *limited.*

6. *Who should draw the line, the boy or the girl?* Theoretically, it is right to say that both the boy and the girl are equally responsible in cooperating together to control their sexual drives until marriage. A couple "going steady" or engaged should agree jointly on a stopping place, and if they slip beyond this limit, they must both use an iron will and fight their way back to self-control, changing the tempting situation immediately. This seems to be reasonable advice. However, there are some serious weaknesses to this thinking in the form of three cold, rigid, stubborn facts that must be faced. *First,* when two young people who think they love each other have the unlimited opportunity to express their

love, there is no natural stopping place. Aroused sexual nature does not know anything about principle, intelligence, reason, an iron will, or anything else but going all the way. *Secondly,* other things being equal, the girl, by nature, has the superior capacity for self-control. It is therefore unrealistic to rest the responsibility for control equally on each. This is not meant to imply that most boys are devoid of principle or self-control. We are discussing the apparatus necessary for sexual control. We must face reality.

Thirdly, it is a fact that it is the girl who runs the risk, who gets pregnant, who has the baby or the abortion. In our society it is the girl who suffers from the social tyranny involved. Therefore, a genuine, positive, realistic program of sexual control until marriage demands that the girl personally set safe limits beyond which she will not go—to state kindly, but firmly, her ideals and intentions when necessary, and to set the pace and control the situation from the first date until marriage.

A tragedy has often been defined as "a sweet and beautiful theory that is murdered by stubborn brutal facts." The idea that both the boy and the girl should draw the line is a sweet and beautiful theory, but the stubborn brutal fact of 350,000 tragedies (babies born out of wedlock) in the United States annually murders this sweet and beautiful theory.

In the final analysis, *the girl must draw the line.* Only *this comes to grips with total reality.* But this does not excuse the man from responsibility, for Biblically he is responsible for carrying out godly principles in the dating life.

7. *Is the desire to marry a virgin a legitimate concern in marriage plans?* In these days of moral revolution and crisis, a few people glibly and gleefully have been asking this question. I have observed that those asking the question are usually characterized by extreme philosophies of secular humanism and materialism. They assume that

man is just a high-grade biological animal. They falsely tend to make "sex" and "love" mean the same thing. They seem to isolate sex as an end-in-itself and to assume that it has no relationship to the other important mental, emotional, social, moral, religious, and aesthetic aspects of total life. These assumptions are out of line with the total realities involved in love, courtship, and marriage relationships. They are false.

The desire for a young man or woman to marry a virgin *is* a legitimate concern in planning marriage, for the following reasons.

(1) The Creator-God planned sex for marriage (Genesis 1:27; 2:25).

(2) The Scriptures refer to sexual intercourse before marriage as being abusive, evil, as being the sin of fornication.

(3) To marry a non-virgin tends to promote suspicion and distrust in marriage. The marriage will tend to be characterized by an uneasiness that there may be extra-sexual permissiveness after marriage.

(4) To marry a virgin tends to promote trust and confidence in marriage. The marriage will tend to be characterized by sexual fidelity.

(5) To marry a virgin tends to indicate that one has married a person who is responsible and trustworthy, who has self-control of his/her own physical urges, who is emotionally and socially mature, who is guided by realistic values and moral judgments, and has respect for the rights of all persons.

(6) To marry a virgin is to marry a person who seems to understand the relationship of sex to total personality and life. He or she understands that "sex is an integral part of the personality. To divide the total entity of an individual into personality and/or sex is like trying to divide . . . society from economics."[7]

[7] J. A. Fritze, *The Essence of Marriage*, Zondervan Publishing House, 1969, p. 95. Used by permission.

(7) To marry a virgin is to marry a person who in all probability is sympathetic to belief in God and basic Christian principles. This fact is described by J. H. Fritze as follows:

> Religion, like sex, is an integral part of the personality. The concepts of a religious belief help to mold the basic traits of a personality and thus mold the sex attitudes of the individual. The value systems in relationship to sex will be formulated by religious convictions. The standards from which one operates in the area of sex will also be governed by religious concepts. In fact, value systems and standards in any area are partially formulated by the force of religion.[8]

To avoid being misunderstood, it is necessary to point out that there are exceptions to the rule of young people marrying a virgin. If a person has repented and received personal forgiveness for past sexual sins, he or she is fully worthy of a Christian marriage. The central core of Christianity is that repentance and confession of sin "makes the wounded whole." Fornication is not the "unpardonable sin" (see Chapter Nine). Also, when a widower marries a widow, neither of them are virgins, but this type of marriage is within the framework of Christian principles.

The idea here is that it is a legitimate concern for young people to want to marry a virgin. Those who deny this ignore the thousands who say in tears, "I'd give anything if I could live that part of my life over again." They ignore the fact that puberty is only the *beginning of adulthood* and that total adulthood and maturity develop later. They ignore the fact that it is important for young people to select their future marriage companions with thoughtful concern and care, yet without a trace of snobbery. They ignore the fact that wise people do not make sex the sole concern in their lives, and that those who do soon become bored with life and often go to an early grave, disillusioned, disappointed, and .defeated.

Sexual promiscuity is contrary to the interests of in-

[8] *Ibid.*, p. 95.

dividual persons and of society. Dr. Hornell Hart sums up the sociological research on this matter when he says:

> We find evidence piling up in our civilization that young people who engage in premarital and extra-marital sexual intercourse *run heavy risks of broken friendships, of unforgettable regrets, of shattered careers, of unsatisfied restlessness, of hideous disease, of social contempt, of disintegrating personalities, and of loss of the deepest and finest love values*[9] (italics added).

8. *Should a couple feel guilty if they by accident go all the way?* What should they do if this one time is the only time they go all the way until marriage? First, we must examine the word "accident." Let us be realistic and inquire kindly: is there really such a thing as a courting couple having sexual intercourse by accident? Probably what this question really means by the term "accident" is that they did not mean to go all the way, but they let their emotions get out of hand and it happened. Frankly now, was it an accident? The answer must be a firm, honest *"No!"* It really happened by both of them willfully and freely making several positive decisions together. They both agreed to seek out a place of privacy where they could be together for a long time, alone. They both agreed to a long period of hugging and kissing, knowing this would develop increased emotional and sexual arousal. They both agreed to light petting—his hands on her body outside her clothing. From there it was but a short step for them both to agree to heavy petting—his hands gradually caressing her body under her clothing, and it was a still shorter step for them both to agree to move from a sitting to a reclining position. Finally they both agreed to go all the way and cooperated in it.

To call this an accident is dishonest rationalization. It is simple self-deception. The cold fact is that both of them had the freedom to stop, to draw the line at

[9] Quoted by Paul Popenoe, "Your Family and You," in *The Knoxville Journal*, July 16, 1969.

any point along the way. Granted, the more they became aroused emotionally and sexually, the less chance there was for moral and religious ideals to operate and the less the possibility for stopping. But it was no accident, and the sooner the couple admit to themselves and to each other that it was not an accident, but that they are equally responsible for their conduct, the easier it will be for them to handle their problem of guilt feeling and sin.

Most Christian couples in love and/or engaged have been tempted many times to go all the way. And yet thousands, yes, millions of fine Christian couples *have* drawn a line, have followed right principles, have used an iron will, and have waited until the total social, moral, and spiritual situation was ready for this matchless one-flesh experience that God our Creator so wonderfully has planned for men and women.

What should a couple do if they go all the way only one time before marriage?

(1) First, they should frankly admit to themselves and to each other their own responsibility for the experience.

(2) They should ask God to forgive them for their sin, to give them leadership and strength that it will not happen again until marriage. One couple told me of going to their church the next day and kneeling at the front and each praying audibly for forgiveness, guidance, and strength. For couples who have gone too far for the first time, I recommend that you read together carefully Chapter Ten of this book, which discusses how to handle guilt feelings and past sexual sins.

(3) Assuming mutual repentance and forgiveness, a couple should not allow this experience to dissolve their courtship. Engagements should be broken only when there are major and basic reasons why personal, social, and spiritual characteristics make a poor marriage risk.

(4) Assuming mutual repentance and forgiveness, continue your courtship and engagement and go ahead with your marriage plans. You should not feel that you

must marry on the sole ground that you were once intimate. This problem has been removed by your repentance and forgiveness. You marry for the same reasons that all others should. You love each other, and you have the personal, social, and spiritual characteristics necessary for a good marriage.

9. *Should an engaged couple confess previous sexual experiences to each other before marriage?* This is a rather complex question, and there is considerable disagreement as to the rightness or wrongness of such confession. Some are quick to say "No!" Others are quick to say "Yes!" Still others are unsure. Judson and Mary Landis, in discussing this problem, state that one should consider the following four important questions before confessing the past:

(1) Why do I feel that I must tell?
(2) Will our marriage be happier if I do tell?
(3) Will my fiance(e) be happier if I tell?
(4) If I must tell, is the fiance(e) the best person to tell it to?[10]

Dr. and Mrs. Landis go on to suggest that if the major purpose of confessing is to relieve strong guilt feeling, it might be better to do the confessing to "a minister, priest or marriage counselor, who can listen and remain silent and undisturbed or is capable of giving wise counsel. . . ."[11] However, the Landises are careful to point out that there are some things that it is necessary to tell the fiance(e), such as having a venereal disease, a child born out of wedlock, a previous marriage, or a prison record.[12]

In addition to the general approach of Dr. and Mrs. Landis, I would suggest that a couple consider the following four questions in deciding whether or not to confess to each other their past sexual sins.

(1) Was the premarital sex experience a one-time affair or was it a continuous pattern over a lengthy period of time?

[10] Landis, *Building a Successful Marriage*, 5th Edition, pp. 241, 242.
[11] *Ibid.*, p. 242.
[12] *Ibid.*, p. 242.

(2) Has the person involved since repented, confessed, and received God's forgiveness?

(3) Is there a possibility that the premarital affair will become known after marriage?

(4) What are the present moral and religious attitudes of my fiance(e)?

Mary Lou came to my office for a private conference. A problem was causing her much concern and she wanted help to do the right thing. Twenty-three years old, she was wearing a diamond ring and bubbling over with joy and happiness about her approaching marriage. She paused and her expression shifted from a happy to a pensive mood.

Then she said, "My problem is this. When I was in high school, at age fifteen, I dated a boy several times. One night we parked and decided to get out and walk. We wandered into the edge of a woods, and one thing led to another and it happened. It was the first time for both of us. It was not a planned affair. We were not Christians, yet we had been brought up in a Christian environment. We talked about it the next day, both of us with strong guilt feelings. He apologized and apologized to me in tears, blaming himself. I told him it was my fault, that I should have stopped us before things got out of control. We agreed never to allow it to happen again and never to tell anyone that it ever happened. The experience caused us gradually to stop dating, yet we continued as trusted friends. Later we became Christians, at different times, he at his church and I at mine. In a few months he was killed in an automobile accident through no fault of his own. At first, my secret inward grief was almost unbearable. But through much prayer I conquered my feelings and looked to the future, determined to live a moral Christian life and plan a Christian marriage. Over seven years have passed, and now I am to be married in a few months."

She stated in glowing terms that her fiance was a fine person and a wonderful Christian. Then, after a pause, she said, "My question to you is, should I tell him of this past experience?" She waited for an answer. I explained that counselors do not make decisions for their counselees but try to help them understand themselves and their social situations so they will be in a position to make their own decisions wisely. Like many students, Mary Lou seemed to expect me to make the decision for her.

Instead, I reasoned with her about the four questions stated above. First, I pointed out that it was a one-time experience and not a continuous pattern of behavior. Second, since the experience both parties had become Christians and received God's complete forgiveness. Third, there was little or no possibility that the experience would ever be known in the future, unless she told it. Then I pointed out that if there were ever cases where one would not confess past sexual sins, her case seemed to be one of them. Finally, I said, "Since your fiance is a Christian, if you do tell him, he would tend to understand, forgive you, and your honesty and sincerity would increase his love for you."

My research among students at a church-related college indicates that eighty-three percent feel that past sexual sins should be discussed with the fiance(e) before marriage. I personally tend to agree with this viewpoint and think that it probably should be discussed during the "engaged-to-be-engaged" period before the engagement is final. One thing is certain, if it is going to be told, it must be told before the wedding night. This honest approach is probably superior to going into marriage without bringing up the matter. Then the guilty party lives with secret guilt feelings and therefore may feel forced later to tell it after marriage. One of the secrets of happy engagements and happy marriages is complete mutual trust, fidelity, and confidence. If and when such a confession is made, a major period of emotional adjustment may follow, especially if the fiance(e) holds to Christian values and has lived a life of self-control. However, if Christian attitudes are followed, other things being equal, the emotional upset can be resolved through forgiveness and understanding, and a happy marriage can follow. Let us remember that wherever and whenever there is sincere sorrow, contrition, and confession of any sin, God's forgiveness is immediate and complete.

In those cases where both parties have been guilty of previous sexual relations, the problem can be resolved through contrition, repentance, confession, and divine forgiveness, plus mutual forgiveness and understanding.

The very fact that there is a major problem involved in whether to tell your fiance(e) or not tell, is another of the many, many reasons why youth should control sex until marriage.

10. *Is it wrong for an engaged couple to look forward anxiously to their sex life in marriage?* Certainly the engagement period ought to be an exceedingly happy time for any couple. But it ought not to be a time when they just mark time waiting for marriage so they can have sex relations and when they angrily criticize society and the church for denying them immediate sex relations. As outlined in chapter eight, the engagement should be a period of natural, active growth and progress. In a genuine engagement, a couple loves each other dearly, and it is their nature to be attracted to each other sexually. It is normal, it is Christian for them to look forward anxiously to the day of their marriage when they can give themselves to each other completely in the God-planned, one-flesh relationship. There should be no guilt feelings on the part of either that they are both anxiously concerned about this. Actually this is a healthy sign. One would worry about any engaged couple who was not eagerly looking forward to sex relations in marriage. Such an attitude would be symptomatic of major personality problems. A couple in this situation should seek help from a qualified counselor before going to the marriage altar.

One day Dora, a shy, quiet, college senior, came to my

office. Her tentative marriage date was a few months away. She explained that she was about to break her engagement. Finally, extremely embarrassed, she was able to say that the problem was her attitude toward sex. She said, "I am deathly afraid of sex. When I think about the first night of our honeymoon, I am mortally horrified. I love John dearly, but I cannot even allow him to kiss me. John has threatened to break our engagement. I know that I ought not to be like this, but I can't seem to do anything about it. I wondered if you would try to help me." During the three conferences that followed I found that her fear of sex had been built up from early childhood by three of her female relatives. They had all had marriage failures and had talked freely before Dora about the wickedness of men and sex until they had gradually conditioned her against marriage, men, and sex. I attempted to help her to understand how she had built up resentment and resistance to sex through her childhood relationships with her relatives and that she should not believe that all men and sex are evil just because these three marriages had failed.

Dora was an eager listener in the conferences. Together we studied passages of Scripture related to sex and marriage, and I was able to help her understand God's purpose for sex in marriage. Finally she brought John with her for a joint conference. I gave them Christian literature on the sexual life in marriage and encouraged them to read it together, which they did. Gradually Dora's false ideas about sex were dispelled, and their marriage took place on the planned date. Six months later Dora came to see me and described her marriage happiness in glowing terms, thanking me repeatedly for helping her out of her confusion. During this visit, one statement she made has stayed with me. In the midst of her happiness she said, "I shudder to think what would have happened in my marriage if I had married with my rebellious and confused attitude toward sex."

Yes, it is normal, it is Christian for engaged couples to anxiously look forward to their sex life in marriage.

CHAPTER 8

HOW TO CONTROL SEX UNTIL MARRIAGE

If sinners entice thee, consent thou not.... My son, walk not thou in the way with them; refrain thy foot from their path: for their feet run to evil.... *(Proverbs 1:10, 15, 16,* KJV)

Blessed is the person who endures trial, for when he stands the test, he will receive the crown of life, which God has promised to those who love Him. No one must say, when he is tempted to do evil, "I have a temptation from God to do evil," for God cannot be tempted to do evil, and He never tempts anyone to do so. But anyone is tempted to do evil when he is allured by his own evil desire and enticed by a bait. The evil desire conceives and gives birth to sin, and when sin is completed, it brings forth death.

(James 1:12-15, Williams)

When I was a young boy, I heard a minister begin his sermon with this sentence: "The wisest person is the one who looks the farthest ahead." Over the years I have had many occasions to think of these words, especially in my work of teaching and counseling with hundreds of young people. I have observed that most young people who misuse and abuse sex indicate that they have little concern for the future.

Although I have been critical of petting on social dates and of premarital sex relations, I am fully aware of the real problems involved in controlling sex during courtship. The Scriptures outline the nature of temptation in simple language. The Apostle Paul says, "So let the man who feels sure of his standing today be careful that he does not fall tomorrow. No temptation has come your way that is too hard for flesh and blood to bear. But God can be trusted not to allow you to suffer any temptation beyond your powers of endurance. He will see to it that every temptation has a way out, so that it will never be impossible for you to bear it" (I Corinthians 10:12, 13, *Phillips*). The Apostle Peter warns, "But you, my friends, whom I love, are forewarned, and should therefore be very careful not to be carried away by the errors of wicked men and so lose your proper foothold. On the contrary, you should grow in grace and in your knowledge of our Lord and saviour Jesus Christ—to him be glory now and until the dawning of the day of eternity" (II Peter 3:17, 18, *Phillips*). James warns us that "A person's temptations are caused by the pull of his own inner evil desires and encouraged by the lure of a convenient social situation. When a person follows his evil desire and takes advantage of the available situation, he or she has sinned. And when sin is allowed to grow and freely run its course, it brings forth death" (a free translation of James 1:13-15). Everyone is blessed by God with sexual drive and concern. The nature of present-day courtship practices—cars, single dates, late hours—furnishes many convenient situations where it would be easy for a person to yield to the pull of his own inner selfish desires and to become involved and overwhelmed physically.

GENERAL SUGGESTIONS
FOR SEXUAL CONTROL DURING COURTSHIP

1. Develop your own positive, basic Christian philosophy about what you believe concerning life, courtship, marriage, and sex. This philosophy should be an individual and a personal one, not merely what you may have read or may have been taught. Group discussions led by the pastor or other church leaders should be helpful to you in forming opinions and answering difficult

questions. (The discussions in chapters one, two, and three may be helpful). Your philosophy must be kept in harmony with basic Christian principles and scientific facts. It needs to be both broad and specific. It should be flexible. As you move through the teens toward adulthood, gradual understanding, experience, and the process of maturing will add new understanding and insights. These insights, when tested by Christian principles and scientific facts, should be added to your Christian life ideals.

2. Set up some rules for courtship conduct that would logically flow from these Christian ideals about life. These rules should be both general and specific. They should be individual, personal, and confidential. It would be helpful to double-check and to reinforce them with one or more principles of one's philosophy of life, one or more Bible passages, and some scientific facts.

3. Select social dates with care. A person should select a date who is similar to himself/herself in age, interests, and ideals. He/she should avoid the type of blind date where both the date and the person arranging the date are complete strangers. A blind date arranged by a close, trusted Christian friend is acceptable. For instance, suppose Marie and Dorothy are close friends, and Dorothy is dating David. Both Dorothy and David are close friends with Ned, but Marie and Ned have never seen or met each other. Dorothy and David suggest arranging a blind date for Marie with Ned. In this case it would be acceptable for Marie to accept the date with Ned because of her complete faith and confidence in Dorothy and David.

4. Plan dates carefully and in advance. They should be creative, interesting, and involve pleasant fellowship. Avoid those dates where there is nothing to do. When a young man and young woman accept a date, they need to understand in advance such facts as where and how they are going, who will be present, what activities

Sexual Understanding Before Marriage

will be engaged in, when and with whom they will be returning.

5. During early courtship days plan dates that involve group participation. Double dates or group dates are recommended, especially during the period of social dating or when dating a person for the first few times. These dates should be planned in conference with parents and in the warm, friendly atmosphere of family life.

6. Strive to be a consistent, devout Christian. Participate actively in the religious life of your church. Plan many dates around the activities of the church. Let the conversation on dates be sprinkled with the language and principles of Christianity. This tends to produce a strong Christian conscience which is the best defense against premarital sex relations. One cannot keep from admiring the young man who said to his fiancee, "I always think of our relationship in terms of 'three'— you, me, and God."

7. Be informed on the subject of sex. A good sex education includes a knowledge of the structure and function of the sexual and reproductive organs and an understanding of the purposes of sex according to the Creator.

8. Avoid those situations and activities that are designed to stimulate and arouse sexual impulses and those things in your private, personal life that would encourage the contemplation of premarital sex relations. This would include such questionable items as sex literature, sex novels, sex movies, and sex photographs. A girl should never go to a boy's apartment or home, or a boy should never go to a girl's apartment or home, when the two are there alone. When a young man arrives to pick up his sweetheart for a date, if no one else is at home, she would not invite him in but would be ready to go when he arrived. This is not to say that a couple should never have any time alone away from the eyes and ears of others. But the habit of long hours in isolated places alone with nothing to do is indicative of poor planning

and questionable motives. It is certainly out of line with a positive program designed to control sexual desires until marriage.

It would be unrealistic to say that the subject of sex should never be mentioned during social dating. On the other hand, it is not a good idea to keep the conversation and jokes sprinkled heavily with sex overtones. In general, it is good during the earlier part of courtship to direct the conversation away from topics associated with this subject. However, there will come times in the average courtship when it is normal and sometimes necessary to allow sex to enter the conversation. During these times, the subject should not be treated with a spirit of prudish dread and panic but with calmness, dignity, and discretion. Of course, when a mature couple is planning marriage, it is necessary for them to discuss privately, frankly, and thoroughly their ideas and attitudes on this subject. But even then it is not necessary that sex constitute a major part of conversation. I recommend that engaged couples planning their marriage should read and discuss my book, *Sexual Happiness in Marriage* (Zondervan, 1967), a few weeks or months before marriage.

9. Avoid the use of intoxicating beverages, and refuse to accept a date with any person who has the habit of using intoxicating beverages. Many irresponsible acts are caused by its influence.

10. Plan to have less frequent dates and to use creative ingenuity to plan enjoyable and more meaningful dates. My recent research among youth at a church-related college indicates that those who date steadily average 3.6 dates per week during the college year. Some couples date every day. This is too often. Both the boy and the girl need time to meet personal needs and to take care of business responsibilities, shopping, laundering, and correspondence, besides needing much time to study. When some time has passed since the last date, the next one can be mutually characterized by a glowing

warmth, a fresh understanding, and a deep appreciation usually not present when couples date too often. Two or three well-planned dates per week will probably make better courtship progress than five or six per week with little or no planning. Some couples date too often and stay out too late. As a result, time weighs heavily on their hands. This is a natural trap to trigger sexual excesses and abuses. Furthermore, they often become bored, not with each other, but with boredom, and arguing and quarreling result.

11. Whenever possible avoid long engagements, especially where a couple can be together every day. Normally when there has been one or two years of courtship before engagement and the couple is of proper age and of proper maturity, long engagements are not necessary. When it is anticipated that a long engagement might be necessary, it would be well to lengthen the social dating period, delay the "going steady" period, and delay the engagement. This should tend to help toward controlling sexual behavior until marriage.

12. During the processes of courtship, both the boy and the girl should keep busy at creative activities. Resorting to creative activities is not just an escape from questionable behavior. Such activities are constructive because they develop personality, self-confidence, and maturity. When our energies are harnessed and channeled in right directions, not only are many positive values produced but such practice also develops self-control of our inner drives and impulses.

In general, courtship decisions and behavior should be guided by reason, intelligence, divine principle, and scientific facts—not by erratic emotions or unbridled selfishness. Courtship must be a triumph of mind over matter, of intelligence over ignorance, of divine principle over human instincts.

Before the marriage ceremony, during the period of "going steady" and engagement, young people need further specific, practical help on their personal courtship relationships, in addition to the general guidelines already mentioned.

One day an honor roll student came to my office for a conference. She was beginning her junior year in college. Her boyfriend was a junior also, and they had been going together for two years and had been engaged for about six months. She related circumstances which made it impossible for them to be married until the summer after graduation, which was nearly two years away. "When couples are in our situation, what can be done to make the waiting easier, especially for the young man?" she asked. A few days later another engaged couple, who were first semester college seniors, sought me out and asked frankly how they could control their emotions until marriage. These two couples are examples of thousands of other fine couples who honestly want to control themselves sexually until marriage, but who are faced with the same agonizing questions. These questions deserve specific answers.

SPECIFIC SUGGESTIONS FOR
SEXUAL CONTROL DURING COURTSHIP

We have discussed in general how to avoid premarital promiscuity. At this point, we will attempt to give *some further practical, specific help to engaged couples,* especially those who have a long waiting period until marriage.

In general, an engaged couple anxious to control themselves until marriage should follow a well-planned program of *sublimation.* Most efforts at sublimation are narrow and limited. A couple will take part in some physical exercise such as tennis or volleyball to drain off some sexual energy. Although this is excellent, it falls pitifully short of total reality. This approach alone seems to indicate that they are simply two animals, and that sex is only a physical something. These assumptions are two of the ugly ideas that are logically deducted from secular materialism. A realistic approach to self-control during engagement is to add to physical sublimation a thorough program of spiritual, mental, and social sublimation. This total program of sublimation would call for a couple's creative ingenuity in planning their lives together. A couple must *get their minds off themselves.* They must *rise above the childish* "I want what I want when I want it" feeling. They must be directed by Christian principle, intelligence, scientific facts, and social truth.

A couple might write out separately and privately their *philosophy of life* on two or three pages and then on a date read them aloud and discuss them. It might be well for them to work out a joint philosophy of life which would be an adjusted combination of the two. This would not be a rigidly binding agreement, but a suggested goal. Such an exercise would help the couple better understand each other, and could prevent them from becoming prisoners of small ideas.

Another suggestion: each might privately select *ten passages from the Bible that would be efficient* guidelines during marriage. Then on a date they could read and discuss the passages together and condense the twenty to ten passages which could be memorized and used as spiritual traffic signs in planning their lives together.

And here is another thought. A couple might write out separately *their life ambitions and goals.* This would include their fondest dreams. Then on a date, or even several dates, read and discuss the two plans thoroughly and work them into one set of goals that would represent what both would like their married life to be. They should ask the Lord to lead them as they gradually work out the plan in their married life.

During the period of engagement a couple could certainly profit by *studying their own personal characteristics and patterns of behavior.* This should not take the form of accusing each other or attempting to force each other to reform. Love does not accuse or force. Basically, this process would be an effort to help them understand themselves and each other. The higher the level of personal maturity before marriage, the greater are the chances for success and happiness. A couple might spend an evening together discussing the *characteristics of individual maturity*. Judson and Mary Landis' description of maturity could be used as a basis for the discussion. The mature person:

(1) Is able to be objective.
(2) Is emotionally independent of parents.
(3) Makes decisions for himself.
(4) Acknowledges and takes responsibility for his mistakes.
(5) Is heterosexual in his sex interests.
(6) Accepts his chronological age.
(7) Is willing to wait for future pleasures.
(8) Profits by his own mistakes.
(9) Accepts the moral codes.
(10) Tries to understand others.
(11) Gets along with other people.
(12) Accepts the present and looks to the future.
(13) Sees sex expression as a normal and satisfying phase.
(14) Is willing to use reason rather than fantasy in courtship.
(15) Can constructively evaluate himself and his motives.[1]

A couple might discuss the subject of *self-control*, not only as it is related to sex, but as it is related to total life experience. What does self-control involve? It involves freedom of choice, right motives, positive action, and present and long-range results and consequences. A study of the following Scriptures will help a couple in planning mutual self-control: Acts 24:16, Romans 6:12, I Corinthians 9:25, and Galatians 5:22, 23.

An engaged couple could explore and utilize the many

[1] Landis, *Building a Successful Marriage*, 3rd Edition, p. 114.

ways in which they can enrich each other's life and express their love to each other aside from bodily contact. There are hundreds of little ways of saying "I love you" that may carry deep meaning. Don't wait for a special occasion to bring a box of candy, a special book, or some flowers to your girl; let her be that special occasion. These events and experiences sometimes become the most cherished and precious moments in your courtship.

Being interested in each other's activities, friends, and family works wonders, making each feel completely included in the other's life.

One of the best ways I know to say "I love you" is to keep yourself as attractive as possible. Men do not like unkempt women, nor do women like sloppy men. With a little extra effort, attractiveness can sometimes put new zing and new life in an otherwise "tired relationship."

Another suggestion: on dates a couple could systematically study together *how to meet problems and situations that normally arise in marriage,* such as, (1) how to handle parent-child relationships; (2) the budgeting of finances; (3) in-law relationships; (4) health imperatives; (5) relationships to the church; (6) social activities, etc. Reading some chapters together out of one of the standard courtship, marriage, and family books (see Bibliography) would be in order.

These activities that I have mentioned are not to be done to the exclusion of others. Elements of concern for each other, proper manners, consideration, compliments, and those special looks are all important ways of saying: "I love you so much, dear."

One engaged couple attempted to improve their vocabulary by studying ten new words each week. Another couple organized groups of teen-agers and held services for some neglected community shut-ins. Still another couple spent considerable time with friends in their courtship struggles, such as helping them to work out double dates and double dating with them when it would be helpful. One couple went to their pastor and volunteered to help wherever they were needed in their church.

During engagement a couple ought to show much interest in and kindness to their parents. Visit and/or write them often. Then there are many other possibilities such as sports (participation and spectator), recitals, plays, operas, and the planning of the wedding. These things are just some examples of spiritual, mental, and social sublimation that will help in sexual self-control until marriage. Let us repeat, these are not just escape mechanisms; they are positive approaches to reality. The main problem of engaged couples is not finding something to do while waiting for marriage, but rather the problem is in finding time to do the many wonderful things that need to be done. In light of the possibilities and potentialities for growth and progress during engagement, it is hard to imagine any couple blaming society because "there isn't anything for young people to do" and for limiting them sexually, so that they fall into the habit of hibernating, spending unlimited hours at drive-in theaters and parking. Such young people are simply reflecting their selfish immaturity.

In the final analysis, to save sex for marriage, a couple must possess some personal Christian maturity, moral discipline, and self-control.

CHAPTER 9

A PROGRAM OF SEXUAL CONTROL
FOR YOUNG MEN: A STUDY OF MASTURBATION

Don't let the world around you squeeze you into its own mould, but let God re-mould your minds from within, so that you may prove in practice that the plan of God for you is good, meets all his demands and moves toward the goal of true maturity. *(Romans 12:2,* Phillips)

Avoid sexual looseness like the plague! Every other sin that a man commits is done outside his own body, but this is an offence against his own body. Have you forgotten that your body is the temple of the Holy Spirit, who lives in you and is God's gift to you, and that you are not the owner of your own body? You have been bought, and at what a price! Therefore bring glory to God in your body.

(I Corinthians 6:18-20, Phillips)

As a teacher of Marriage and Family classes, I have practiced having separate meetings of men and women during the last two class periods each semester. Both men and women are asked to write out in advance questions for discussion in these meetings. They do not sign their names. The class period consists of a practical candid discussion of their personal questions and the problems involved. During one such meeting, a married male student submitted the following question for discussion: "You may not consider this important, but I would like you to discuss the issue of masturbation of both single and married men. Should a married man go without sexual intercourse indefinitely without masturbation? The main issue here is, is the sin question involved?"

In this chapter I want to have a frank and detailed discussion with young men on the subject of "sexual control until marriage," using the honest question of this young man as a launching pad. I say, in genuine sincerity, that this problem of sexual control may be *the* major problem that young men have to face from puberty until marriage. The Christian community has avoided far too long an open confrontation with this question. Our silence has often been unchristian, cowardly, and sometimes deadly. We have abandoned many fine young men to the mercy of their own lusts, anxieties, and guilt feelings.

There are three important topics that the young man wanted discussed: what about single men practicing masturbation; what about married men practicing masturbation on some occasions; and is masturbation a sin? These three questions are honest, and courageous. They deserve honest and frank answers.

THE BIOLOGICAL DYNAMIC OF THE MALE SEXUAL DRIVE

To help young men understand themselves and the physical and psychological dynamics (factors) related to masturbation, let us focus our thoughts on (1) the nature and structure of these dynamics and (2) the history of the Christian community's effort to interpret them.

In a healthy youth each gonad continually manufactures sperm cells and sends them out into the epididymis. The epididymis is a coiled tube attached to the top of each gonad. It is in reality a temporary storage tank for the sperm cells. As this storage tank is filled, the sperm is moved out of each epididymis through each vas deferens into the body cavity and lodged in two other internal body storage tanks called the seminal vesicles. When the seminal vesicles are filled, the sexual drive of the person comes alive and is ripe for release.

It is necessary to say that the male sex drive is not just a biological thing "hinging" upon sperm production and release. If this were the case, how sad life would be for both male and female. The male sex drive is also mental, emotional, and spiritual. Yet, the biological dynamic of the male sex drive is real. The mature Christian must face the fact that nature demands a release.

As the gonads continue the process of producing sperm, *the semen* (sperm plus fluids) *must go somewhere. An ejaculation of some kind is necessary. God created men thus.* In our research involving 151 young married men we asked the question, "How often would you like to have sex relations and an orgasm if you could have this experience every time you really wanted to?" Their response was every 2.7 days. This illustrates the biological dynamic of the male sex drive.

What has been the Christian advice to young men regarding the problem of their sex drive before marriage? Historically, there have been two main approaches. At one extreme, certain liberal thinkers, advocating a materialistic viewpoint, recommend regular masturbation as a normal part of the maturing process. These people usually refuse to distinguish between various types of masturbation. They largely take the New Morality approach and leave it up to the individual to decide what is right and what is wrong. There is little or no effort to relate the problem to the Bible or basic Christian principles. Being rather humanistic in their thinking, their emphasis is upon the physical dynamic of human nature, and they largely neglect the emotional, the moral, and the spiritual aspects of this behavior. They often state or imply that masturbation is one of the blessings of God to young men.

At the other extreme are those who teach or imply that "all masturbation is evil." They hold that masturbation is selfish, childish, and will result in emotionally disturbed personalities. They quote Scripture to prove that all masturbation is evil and opposed to the will of

God. This approach emphasizes the emotional, moral, and spiritual aspects of this behavior and tends to ignore the physical nature of young men. These people, consciously or unconsciously, tend to allow their semi-ascetic assumptions to determine what is right and what is wrong, and they read these assumptions into the Holy Scriptures.

Both of these approaches rest upon an isolated part-truth. On the one hand, the physical dynamic of the male sex nature is God-created. It is not evil. But man is far more than a mere biological creature. To treat him as such is both unchristian and irrational; it is materialistic. There is not a trace of this type of materialistic doctrine in either the Old or New Testament. On the other hand, man (and woman), created in the image of God, is a non-material self, a soul, a person, an agent. He is self-conscious and has self-knowledge and self-control. He can remember the past, plan the future, accept responsibility, hold values, experience interaction with other persons, and exercise faith in God. The core of human nature is non-material. Thus, man is both spirit and flesh, and God made him that way. To state, to assume, or to imply that the spirit of man is good and the body is evil is to sanction the ascetic dualism of the early Greeks and Persians. There is not a trace of ascetic dualism in either the Old or New Testament.

Body and spirit work together in direct interaction as a unit, as opposed to their being hostile enemies as these two extreme viewpoints indicate. Neither of these viewpoints consider fairly and fully the total human person.

THE PSYCHOLOGICAL DYNAMIC
OF THE MALE SEX DRIVE

The psychological dynamic of the male sex drive flows from the nature of the physical dynamic and the two extreme interpretations, the materialistic and the ascetic. In this materialistic-ascetic dilemma, what is a boy to do? If he tends to be independent, rebellious, and to follow the crowd, he will probably heed the materialistic point of view and accept the idea that "masturbation is in no way sinful." Thus he will probably form the habit of excessive masturbation, and this may lead to fantasy and to premarital sex relations. It is a short step from saying that "no masturbation is sinful" to saying that "sexual promiscuity is good." Furthermore, his habit of masturbation and his ideas about sexual promiscuity may become a major stumbling block to a successful marriage.

On the other hand, if a boy respects the values of his family and society, he will probably accept the view that "all masturbation is sinful." He accepts this idea as truth and resolves to avoid masturbation. When he hears such passages as "keep thyself pure" and "abstain from all appearances of evil," he resolves to do so, yet he struggles with the continuous pressure of his strong sex drive as he grows older. If he yields to the dynamic pressure of his sex drive by releasing it through masturbation, he struggles with his conscience and guilt feelings as a consequence. He gradually becomes confused and wonders about God, the church, and religious teachings. This promotes lack of self-confidence and insecurity, and it may develop into personality problems. These attitudes and inner feelings do not constitute a normal foundation for a stable marriage.

Most young men want to do right, but in their youth the complex blessing of human sexuality is not easily understood. The sex drive demands release. The young man finds himself in the midst of an intense struggle. Under these circumstances, what should he do?

Because of this dilemma, I have felt for many years that young men need an interpretation of sex from a Christian point of view—a balanced Christian approach concerning sexual self-control until marriage.

God created you to be a total person with mental, emotional, spiritual, and physical natures. Closely related to and integrated with your mental, emotional, and spiritual natures is your God-created physical nature, including your sexual nature. And part of a man's physical nature is his *strong* sex drive that repeatedly calls for expression. It is only honest to admit that young men *do* have a major problem with sexual self-control.

Dr. Lofton Hudson tells of a young man who came to his office for a personal conference. The boy told Dr. Hudson that he had a major problem; he thought no one else had such a major problem as he did in controlling his sexual drives. Dr. Hudson commended the young man for seeking help with his problem, but kindly corrected the boy's assumption that he was the only young man who had a problem with sexual control. The counselor pointed out that other young men also have the same sexual problems and temptations.

Although the sexuality of man is a strong drive that is rather difficult to control, it is, on the other hand, a wonderful blessing, indeed. It is such a superior human blessing that we ought not only to express our gratitude to God for it, but we ought to be concerned about controlling it and using it in our lives according to God's creative purpose for it.

Having called attention to the facts (1) that we have a strong sex drive, (2) that other men are like us and wrestle with the problem of sexual control just as we do, and (3) that our sexuality is one of our major human blessings, we are now ready to face frankly the question: how should young men control their sexual drive until marriage? In the early years after puberty (approximately thirteen to seventeen), a young man does not normally have a major problem of sexual self-control. But he gradually develops sexually until he reaches a peak in sexual drive at age nineteen. Thus in the late adolescent years until marriage, his strong sex drive urgently calls for expression and release. What are the possible alternatives or choices available to a young man?

(1) He may marry and receive release from his strong sexual drive through normal sexual intercourse with his

wife. However, early marriage for the sole purpose of meeting the sex drive is not recommended.

(2) He may remain single and meet his sexual needs through promiscuous sex relations with women.

(3) He may meet his sexual need through homosexuality, that is, practicing sexual stimulation with members of his own sex.

(4) He may depend upon nocturnal seminal emissions for release and control of his strong sex drive. The word "nocturnal" means "night" or "occurring at night." The intelligent Creator, who gave boys their strong sex drive, also gave them an automatic built-in sexual release. That is, at night during sleep a boy experiences sexual orgasm, that is an ejaculation of semen which gives a sexual release.

(5) He may use sublimation. This is the process of draining off and burning up sexual desire through physical and mental exercise, activities, and projects.

(6) He may practice masturbation or what is technically called "autoeroticism." The word "auto" means "self" and "eroticism" means "sexual stimulation." Thus, masturbation means "self sexual stimulation."

It is obvious that the ultimate plan of our Creator is for a young man to meet his sexual need through marriage (Proverbs 5:1-23, Matthew 19:4-6, I Corinthians 7:2-5, I Thessalonians 4:1-8). But let us imagine a mature young man who has reached his sexual peak but, due to circumstances beyond his control, must put off marriage for a few years. How is he to control his sex drive until marriage? In Chapters Four and Seven we concluded that it is necessary to reject sexual intercourse by a single man with any woman as being the sin of fornication or immorality (II Samuel 13:12-15, Proverbs 5:1-19, I Corinthians 6:13-20, Ephesians 5:1-11).

Also, historic Christianity has rejected all forms of homosexuality as being immoral. Paul, in writing to the Christians at Rome, discussing the evils of homosexuality, said, "God therefore handed them over to disgrace-

ful passions. Their women exchanged the normal practices of sexual intercourse for something which is abnormal and unnatural. Similarly the men, turning from
natural intercourse with women, were swept into lustful
passions for one another. Men with men performed
these shameful horrors, receiving, of course, in their
own personalities the consequences of sexual perversity.
Moreover, since they considered themselves too high
and mighty to acknowledge God, he allowed them to
become the slaves of their degenerate minds..." (Romans 1:26-28, *Phillips*). Homosexuality is an abnormal
practice that is a sin against God and His purpose for
life. It is a sin against the other person involved. It
destroys the normal functions of life and erodes and
deforms personality development. Reason, intelligence,
common sense, and Christian principles should lead any
man (or woman) to reject homosexuality as an acceptable means of meeting sexual needs.

To say that homosexuals are "sick" people is to state
a part-truth, at best. The rest of the truth is that, in the
beginning, the homosexual was a free person who simply
made bad choices and evil decisions, when he knew
better. *It was his willful evil choices that made him a
sick person.* Indeed, he is a sick person who needs Christian sympathy, divine forgiveness, and psychiatric help.
But the assumption that a homosexual has a compulsion,
caused by society, over which he has no control, has
to be rejected. Many others who have had the same
strong drives and have grown up in the same society
with similar family backgrounds have freely, yet firmly,
rejected temptations to homosexuality. The practicing
homosexual is a sinner against God and man and in due
process develops into a sick person. This is not meant
to ignore the fact that personality development is influenced by environment, but it is intended to deny
that the individual is *mechanically* determined by his
environment.

Since the single young man must reject both sexual

promiscuity and homosexuality, this leaves only three alternatives open to him, namely, nocturnal emissions, sublimations, and masturbation. *I recommend that a young man lean on nocturnal emissions as a basic method of release from his strong sex drive. This is possible; many have done so.* In addition, I recommend sublimation as a helpful means of sexual control. A young man can drain off much of his sexual energy through planned physical exercises, personal hobbies, and social activities and projects that help him keep busy, happy, and content.

As we have said, during a boy's early years of puberty, controlling the sexual drive need not be a major problem. It is only when he becomes *preoccupied* with his sexual nature that sex becomes a major problem. However, when a young man approaches his peak in sexual drive at age nineteen, his problem of sexual control gradually becomes more and more difficult. Approximately five percent of men this age never experience nocturnal emissions. This tends to complicate the problem of sexual control for these young men. For others nocturnal emissions are slow in triggering the needed release.

WHEN IS MASTURBATION SINFUL?

Before discussing the circumstances under which masturbation is not sinful, let us examine carefully the question, "When is masturbation sinful?" It is sinful (1) when its sole motive is sheer biological pleasure unrelated to anything else, (2) when one allows it to become a compulsive habit which controls his person, or (3) when the habit results from inferior feelings and causes guilt feelings. The sin in these cases involves a violation of divine principles. Those persons who practice masturbation with these motives are in need of sympathetic understanding from parents and counseling from qualified professional people such as pastors, marriage counselors, doctors, psychologists, and psychiatrists.

Masturbation is also sinful when, during the act, a young man opens a pornographic or sensual magazine and imagines he is having relations with the nude person pictured. It is sinful if a boy, during the act, recalls a beautiful girl he saw recently and imagines in fantasy he is having sex relations with her. These illustrations of fantasy constitute brazen lust. The boy involved is simply using sex as a means to his own personal enjoyment. He is guilty of adultery. Jesus said, "Whosoever looketh on a woman to lust after her hath committed adultery with her already in his heart" (Matthew 5:28). In these cases, looking at a picture and lusting through fantasy with an imaginary or a real woman is adultery. The sin in such cases involves both a violation of Christian principles and a violation of another person in one's heart.

WHEN IS MASTURBATION NOT SINFUL?

Now let us examine, carefully, the question, "When is masturbation not sinful?" In the past, much of the Christian community has been rather rigid and dogmatic in saying that all masturbation is sinful and that all boys should control themselves without any form of sexual release, other than nocturnal emissions, until marriage. Some have even referred to nocturnal emissions as being sinful. When we consider the strong, urgent sexual drive of the single young man who has reached the peak of his sexual drive, we feel that a rigid condemnation of all masturbation as being sinful is rather arbitrary, unrealistic, and out of harmony with the creative plan of God. We feel that the Christian community needs to take a *long hard look* at this attitude and understand that we should be more realistic in our teaching.

After a young man has honestly tried to depend on nocturnal emissions and sublimation to control his sex drive, the fact remains that these are not sufficient for some young men for sexual self-control until marriage at age 21-25. The Christian community must come to grips with this "nitty-gritty" reality. The Christian response to this problem may well determine the spiritual, moral, and social attitudes and the future of many fine young men. We must teach that it is within the Christian understanding of God's plan and purpose for a young man's life that he may practice, without being sinful, a *limited, temporary program of masturbation* from the time he approaches a peak in his sexual drive until he is married. In other words, we are saying that a man should practice *sexual self-control* until marriage. *He must never violate another person* to meet his sexual needs. He *must* lean on nocturnal emissions and sublimation and he *may*, when needed, supplement them with a temporary, limited program of masturbation. Please, note the emphasis here is *self-control* in order to avoid yielding to the temptations of immorality. Also, please note the use of the words *limited* and *temporary*. Let us assume that the *sole motive* of such masturbation is for the purpose of self-control until marriage. The boy is fully committed to the idea of living a pure life until marriage. In the process of resorting to occasional masturbation he can anchor his thinking on such Biblical principles as: God created me with a strong sex drive (Genesis 1:27); God created me for marriage (Mark 10:6-8); God expects me to practice sexual self-control until marriage (Romans 6:12; I Corinthians 9:25; Titus 1:15); and it is God's purpose that I give myself through His divinely planned family life to sacrificial, Christian service that is outgoing and creative (Mark 8:34-37; Romans 12:1, 2, 9-21). Before or after the act a boy can breathe a prayer to God such as: "Thank You, Lord, for the wonderful blessings of life and of sex. Help me to practice self-control until marriage. May I never violate a person or Your will." If a man is engaged to be married, his attitude and prayer could be saturated with thanksgiving for his fiancee and petitions that he keep himself pure and worthy of her in marriage. Certainly he would not allow himself to drift into lustful fantasy imagining that he is having sex relations with her. Yet it is normal for him to look forward to having sex relations with his fiancee in marriage, and at the same time realize that he does not desire premarital sex relations with her. If the idea of prayer in connection with limited masturbation is upsetting to the reader, maybe we should remind ourselves that, in the Christian life, prayer and solving life's problems go together. Paul did not hesitate to combine prayer and sexual control (I Corinthians 7:5). As stated in Appendix I, Jesus determined right and wrong in terms of the inward condition (motives) of the heart. Let us not overlook the fact that basic to our discussion is the idea that right motives directed by Christian principles indicate right acts. In this case *the motive is not lust, but self-control.* To overlook this is to miss the point of this discussion.

What is the result of a limited program of masturbation for the purpose of self-control? Of course, there is the needed physical release, accompanied with physical pleasure. But the sole purpose of the act is self-control, not pleasure. This has no harmful physical effects and no person has been violated. Thus the major result is the boy's personal, moral, and spiritual satisfaction in knowing that he is striving for the mastery of himself through a program of self-control. Within this framework of proper motives, there are no evil results. Thus we may say that *when masturbation is practiced on a limited basis for the sole purpose of self-control, when it is guided by basic Christian principles, and has no evil results, it is an acceptable act. It is not lust. It should not be followed by guilt feelings.*

Let us digress a moment and relate the above principles to a married man in answer to the original question raised at the beginning of this chapter. Suppose a man has been married ten years and has experienced a normal, healthy sex life with his wife with average frequency of sex relations twice per week. Note that for ten years he has had no need for other sexual outlets, such as nocturnal emissions or masturbation. Now suppose his wife has to spend two months at the bedside of her sick mother hundreds of miles away. He must stay at home to keep the children in school and continue his occupational responsibilities. During this time his healthy sexual needs remain constant. In spite of his efforts at sublimation and control, his sexual needs speak urgently. There is nothing wrong with his practicing a limited program of masturbation in the spirit described above, breathing a prayer of thanksgiving for his wonderful wife and requesting strength to remain sexually faithful to his wife and worthy of her love. This procedure is not lust. It is not sinful. It is within the framework of basic Christian principles. It is acceptable behavior. There is no reason why a married man in this situation should feel guilty about his behavior.

Or consider a second example where a man cannot have any sexual relations with his wife from four to six weeks before and after the birth of a child. Here a span of two to three months (or longer in some cases) passes with no way for the husband to have a sexual release. This is a difficult time of adjustment for the father because of changes in the home and family. Often someone comes to live in the home for a time to help in caring for the new baby and the mother; there is now a new love object; and physically his wife is unable to have intercourse at a time when he would greatly like to share his love with and for her. At this time men are extremely vulnerable and are often tempted to look elsewhere for a sexual release. This can result in marital infidelity, which could have been averted had there been a sexual release. In this case it would be good for the couple to stimulate each other to orgasm without intercourse. Many couples even use this normal procedure during the menstrual period. However, when circumstances do not permit this, masturbation as described above would be a helpful alternative.

Although we are talking about masturbation prior to marriage for self-control, a word about masturbation in childhood is also in order. Most Christian pastors, counselors, and leaders would agree with William Graham Cole who says:

> If it is taken for granted that the child should explore and experiment with all parts of his body, he accepts his sexual organs as casually as his fingers and toes.... Parental attitudes toward [child] masturbation are especially important.... The Christian acceptance of the body has an important place in the training of the young. Children should be taught to value and appreciate their bodies.... Continued and habitual masturbation which is compulsive indicates an inner emotional disturbance, the need for love, understanding, support, reassurance. Patient attempts to discover the source of the problem and to deal with that instead of its symptoms will prove the only adequate approach.[1]

In the past boys have been warned by adults that masturbation would cause them to become sterile, would cause them to be feeble-minded, and would cause their children to become feeble-minded. Doctors and biologists today would call all such ideas pure superstition. There is no scientific evidence that masturbation is biologically harmful.

GUILT FEELINGS

Since many young men have suffered untold agony in guilt feelings about masturbation, it is in order to discuss the nature of guilt feelings and how to deal with them. Guilt feelings are the mental and emotional conditions of a person who has violated or thinks he has violated some divine, natural, or social law and blames and condemns himself for these acts.

Animals (cats, dogs, etc.) seem to know little or nothing about sin, right and wrong, or guilt feelings. Man (and woman), created in the image of God, is unique in that he has many mental and emotional characteristics

[1] William Graham Cole, *Sex in Christianity and Psychoanalysis*, Oxford University Press, 1955, pp. 318, 319.

not found in animals.[2] One of these characteristics is guilt feelings.

Guilt feelings *are* real. They are *universal* in the lives of men and women. They are inherent in human nature. The Bible teaches that guilt feelings are the result of man's rebellion against God and the violation of His will and His moral and natural law. To state it simply, guilt feelings result from sin—sin against God. The following are a few of the many passages which indicate that the Bible teaches that man is sinful by nature.

1. "For there is not a just man upon earth, that doeth good, and sinneth not." (Ecclesiastes 7:20)
2. "But we are all as an unclean thing, and all our righteousnesses are as filthy rags." (Isaiah 64:6)
3. "Ye are of your father the devil, and the lusts of your father ye will do." (John 8:44)
4. "For all have sinned, and come short of the glory of God" (Romans 3:23)
5. "If we say that we have no sin, we deceive ourselves, and the truth is not in us." (I John 1:8)

In like manner the Bible teaches that when a person sins, inner guilt feelings follow his sins. Paul tells us that the Gentiles have the law of God written in their hearts and that, when they sin, their consciences verify the existence of the law and condemn their behavior (Romans 2:14, 15). A clear Biblical example of guilt feelings following a sin is found in Psalm 51. David, king of Israel, had committed adultery with Bathsheba, the wife of Uriah, a soldier in Israel's army. To cover his sin, David gave orders that Uriah be sent to the front in an active military battle, and Uriah was killed in the battle.

[2] Sociologist Charles H. Cooley called these characteristics "human sentiments." He defined them as those mental and emotional impulses (1) that develop in human beings in social interaction in society, (2) that are superior to the mental and emotional impulses of lower animals, (3) that belong to the total human race, and (4) that are not peculiar to any culture, race, or time. Examples of these mental and emotional impulses are sympathy, love, pride, laughter, ambition, intellectual curiosity, modesty, hero-worship, group identification, the feeling of right and wrong, and *guilt feelings*.

Thus David, who had been a good man in years past, was now guilty of adultery and murder. The intense anguish and agony of David's guilt feelings are expressed in beautiful poetry in Psalm 51. He cries out, "Have mercy upon me, O God. . . . My sin is ever before me. . . . Hide thy face from my sins, and blot out all mine iniquities. Create in me a clean heart, O God. . . ." Any person who is suffering from guilt feelings over past sexual sin, or any sin, would do well to read this psalm over and over again.

To be sure, evil people can gradually train their consciences and commit sins with little or no guilt feelings, but this often takes many years and is the exception, not the rule.

How should youth (and adults) handle guilt feelings? There are four possible approaches:

1. Rationalize and reason with yourself that your guilt feelings are not there—that they do not really exist. They are inventions of society and narrow-minded religious fanatics. Be brave, courageous, aggressive. Try to impress your peers that your sinfulness is a normal healthy behavior, that your individual life constitutes real happiness and real living. In general, this is, in part, the approach of Sigmund Freud. He attempted to reduce the power of society (the superego) and to increase the strength of the individual self (the ego).[3] This approach is like denying the existence of a dangerous infection or disease.

2. A second approach to guilt feelings is to repress them; that is, since they are painful to you, drive them out of your *conscious* mind into your *subconscious* mind. In simple language, just refuse to think about them. But this does not solve the problem. The guilt feelings are still in existence. Your daily life experiences with people remind you of your sins and cause your guilt feelings to surface, to move back into your stream

[3] Harold W. Darling, *Man in Triumph,* Zondervan Publishing House, 1969, p. 34. Used by permission.

of conscious thought. Thus, the painful guilt feelings have to be driven back again into your subconscious mind. This vicious cycle continues, and seems to increase in speed and intensity. It is obvious that this approach to your guilt feelings will promote major emotional problems.

3. A third approach to guilt feelings is to admit them, refuse to forgive yourself, and hate yourself. In so doing, you live in the past and neglect and paralyze your future. You promote your own hostility, anxiety, and despair. Darling says, "Some of us are unable to forgive ourselves for our past sins, and dwell morbidly upon them. ... We foster within ourselves a need for self-punishment, as if we could somehow atone for our own sins by our own suffering. ... To refuse to forgive ourselves is not only spiritually damaging; it displays a distrust in God's work in our lives, a misconception of the nature of God, as well as a lack of faith."[4] It is obvious that self-hatred because of guilt feelings over our sins can do untold damage to our mental, emotional, and spiritual lives.

4. Finally, the Christian approach to guilt feelings over sin is to admit to ourselves that "The prime source of our guilt lies in a broken relationship with God and our fellowman, through the separating element of sin."[5] Instead of punishing ourselves through agonizing guilt feelings, we should do four things:

a. In a spirit of sorrow, regret, and humble contrition we should repent of our sins; that is, we should reverse our mind and attitude toward sin. We should admit to ourselves that sinful behavior is against God, and we should, therefore, turn our back upon it (Psalm 51:17; Isaiah 55:6; Ezekiel 18:31; Mark 2:17; Luke 15:7).

b. We should confess our sins to God and ask for His divine forgiveness (Luke 15:18; I John 1:9).

c. We should by faith in the person and work of

4 *Ibid.*, p. 58.
5 *Ibid.*, p. 56.

Jesus Christ, through His death on the cross, receive God's complete forgiveness (Romans 1:17, 3:28, 5:1; I Timothy 6:12; Hebrews 10:22).

d. After we have received the fullness of God's forgiveness, we must become involved in aggressive action in Christian witnessing and living. To the best of our ability, and with the leadership of the Holy Spirit, we must live the Christian life (Luke 9:25; Romans 12:1; Galatians 5:13; James 2:17, 22).

Now, let us apply these ideas about guilt feelings to masturbation. If a young man practices a limited program of masturbation for the sole purpose of sexual self-control, as described above, there is no reason why he should have guilt feelings. On the other hand, if he has practiced masturbation for personal physical pleasure as an end in itself, accompanied by fantasy, guilt feelings would normally accompany such practice. We need to remember that we get rid of our guilt feelings related to sexual sin in the same way that we get rid of guilt feelings related to any sin. Also, we should remember that, after we have confessed our sins and received God's complete forgiveness and our guilt feelings are fully relieved, we should be on our guard, lest we fall back into the old patterns of behavior. We will still have our same sexual drives and needs, and there will be many subtle temptations to lure us back into sin. An active, aggressive creative life of Christian witnessing and living is the best defense against falling back into old sinful habits. When we feel weak in the face of our sex-saturated, permissive society, let us remember (1) that "God can be trusted not to allow you to suffer any temptation beyond your powers of endurance" (I Corinthians 10:13, *Phillips*); and (2) that God's leadership and grace are sufficient for us, and that His strength is often made perfect through our weakness (II Corinthians 12:9). The question of how to deal with past sexual sins will be discussed more fully in Chapter Eleven.

THE BIBLE AND MASTURBATION

Let us now consider some of the criticisms that may be brought against the idea that under some circumstances masturbation is not sinful.

Some readers may object on the grounds that the Bible condemns all masturbation as being sinful. This assumption needs careful examination. The two Bible passages usually used as proof texts to condemn all masturbation as being sinful are Genesis 38:8-11 and I Corinthians 6:9, 10. In the Genesis passage two short statements are lifted out of context and interpreted as a universal condemnation of masturbation. The two statements are "he spilled it [his semen] on the ground" (verse 9) and "the thing which he did displeased the Lord" (verse 10). Many sincere, well-meaning people have used these statements out of context as an absolute condemnation of all masturbation. In a careful reading of the passage we are told that when Onan's older brother Er died, his father Judah instructed Onan to marry Tamar, the wife of his deceased brother, and raise up children to her, according to the traditional practice of the Hebrews. When Onan had intercourse with Tamar, he practiced "coitus interruptus," that is, he withdrew before orgasm, spilling his semen on the ground. The thing that displeased the Lord was Onan's refusal to carry out his moral duty and raise up children to his deceased brother's wife, according to Hebrew custom. It is obvious that masturbation is not involved in any way in this passage.

The other passage, I Corinthians 6:9, 10, reads as follows: "Know ye not that the unrighteous shall not inherit the kingdom of God? Be not deceived: neither fornicators, nor idolators, nor adulterers, nor effeminate, nor abusers of themselves with mankind, nor thieves, nor covetous, nor drunkards, nor revilers, nor extortioners, shall inherit the kingdom of God."

In the past, these same sincere, well-meaning people have lifted the words "abusers of themselves with mankind" out of verse 9 and have interpreted them to mean people who masturbate. This makes masturbation a sin equal to such sins as fornication, adultery, stealing, and drunkenness. This interpretation is false. The words "abusers of themselves with mankind" mean "homosexuals." The passage simply does not deal with the topic of masturbation.

It is significant that both the Old and the New Testaments are silent on the subject of masturbation. Certainly Christians should be careful about basing major beliefs or major decisions on the absence of Biblical instructions. Yet, the Bible cannot give detailed instructions about all possible human actions or behaviors. Masturbation is such an act. In this and similar cases, it is necessary to apply broad Biblically based principles to the behavior involved in order to determine whether the act is right or wrong.

Could it be that one reason why the Christian community has failed to apply basic Christian principles to the subject of masturbation is because of the fact that the Bible is silent on the subject?

MASTURBATION AND FANTASY

The reader may be rejecting the reasoning of this chapter on two other grounds: (1) It is impossible for a young man to masturbate without fantasy, that is, without thinking about or imagining and associating his masturbation with having sex relations with some known or imaginary girl; (2) since it is impossible to masturbate without such fantasy, then it is true that all masturbation violates the principles set out in Jesus' statement: "Whosoever looketh on a woman to lust after her hath committed adultery with her already in his heart" (Matthew 5:28).

As stated above, I certainly agree that all masturbation accompanied with such fantasy *is* a violation of Matthew 5:28. Furthermore, it is a violation of the tenth commandment, "Thou shalt not covet." I would also agree that much masturbation *is* accompanied by such fantasy and is, therefore, evil. However, I must reject the premise that it is impossible to masturbate without fantasy. We cannot consider the male nocturnal emission as being evil, and yet it is a divinely planned sexual release that does not involve the opposite sex, neither is it lust because it does not involve the conscious mind. Furthermore, when a single male who is nineteen or more has gone for several days without any kind of sexual release, his two sperm reservoirs (epididymis and the seminal vesicles) are filled with sperm (semen). At this point the male sex drive is very strong, is easily aroused, and demands release. The stimulation given by masturbation quickly produces the release. With self-control as the sole motive, this process is not lust.

I insist that this experience is possible without fantasy and without lust. God has created us in His image and has given us the capacity and the freedom to accept or reject evil thoughts. The regenerated Christian, directed by Christian ideals and led by the Holy Spirit, can train himself to reject evil thoughts. The person who insists that it is impossible for any man to masturbate without fantasy is unconsciously assuming that if an evil thought comes into a person's mind during masturbation, he has violated Matthew 5:28. This is simply not true. All of us know that it is impossible for us to keep evil thoughts from entering our minds. Also, we know that it is possible for us to reject evil thoughts and drive them out of our minds. Sin is not anchored in the fact that an evil thought may enter our minds, but rather it is anchored in the practice of *deliberately accepting, encouraging,* and *entertaining evil thoughts.* On this point, I well remember that while I was a teen-ager my Sunday school teacher used to say, "We cannot keep the birds from flying over our heads, but we can keep them from building nests in our hair." We *can* control our thoughts if we want to do so. When a young man walks down the street and sees a beautiful girl dressed in an immodest mini-skirt, evil thoughts can automatically flash into his mind. He can easily entertain these evil thoughts, or he can reject them and think pure thoughts.

Dr. M. D. Hugen has a rather heavy but masterful discussion on the distinction between *involuntary* sexual mental images and desires and *voluntary* sexual mental images and desires.[6] The word involuntary refers to desires and mental images that are automatic and appear in our minds without willful thought. The word voluntary refers to desires and mental images that result from our willful thoughts, choices, and decisions. Dr. Hugen points out that involuntary mental images are not the same as voluntary mental images. They arise as the result of "association" with persons, ideas, words, and social situations. Thus, the involuntary mental images involving sex are not sinful. They are a part of the nature of man. Furthermore, it is wrong to deny their existence; to do so will result in guilt feelings and major problems of sexual control.

Thus, when the young man sees the girl with an extreme mini-skirt, by association there automatically arise within him desires and mental images with sexual overtones. As Dr. Hugen points out, "these automatic desires and mental images are . . . not the same as thoughts. In thinking, the person, the 'I' in the narrow sense of the responsible religious center of man, is involved. . . . The distinction is readily evident in an example: The word adultery produces a mental image of a sinful sex act. The mental image is neither moral nor religious [nor immoral or irreligious]. It is even necessary for the understanding of the seventh commandment. The person's attitude or response to this mental image *is moral, not neutral* or *natural. This mental process may be sinful* (italics added)."[7]

We should note that Matthew 5:28 states that a man who lusts (continues to lust) after a woman has already

[6] M. D. Hugen, *The Church's Ministry to the Older Unmarried*, William B. Eerdmans Publishing Company, 1959, pp. 99-102.
[7] *Ibid.*, pp. 101-102.

committed adultery with her *in his heart*. Where is the adultery located? In his heart, that is, in his mind, will, purpose, and motives. A boy who uses a *limited* program of masturbation *without fantasy for the sole purpose of self-control* is willfully avoiding adultery in his heart or in an act. If a young man follows the limited program of masturbation suggested above, he will have no problem in transferring to normal healthy heterosexual relations in marriage without any guilt feelings or emotional problems. His healthy pre-marital attitudes and motives will make this possible. However, if a young man practices *excessive* masturbation for pleasure and with fantasy before marriage, we may well expect that as soon as the newness of marriage has worn off that he may in fantasy imagine sexual intimacy with someone other than his wife and, therefore, be guilty of adultery in his heart. The more he thinks of a relationship with another, the more likely he will be to have a poor relationship with his wife. This in turn could trigger more thoughts of fantasy and a marriage could collapse. And all because the husband entertained deep feelings of fantasy and lust before marriage.

Some readers may say that when we take a position advocating a middle-of-the-road suggestion of limited masturbation for the purpose of self-control, we invite criticism from both sides. This may be true, but it is necessary to reply, "So what?" As long as these two extreme interpretations (1) do not rest upon basic Biblical principles, (2) tend toward results involving possible major personal problems, and (3) do not meet the God-created needs of young men as total persons, it is not necessary to worry about such criticism. Young men need to understand that these two extreme positions present major problems for them. They need the truth contained in both of these views, but not as taken to their extremes.

Other readers may say that to advocate a limited amount of masturbation for the purpose of self-control is to "violate one's self." A careful reading of the above pages will reveal that the motives of occasional masturbation are to control one's sexual drive, to keep self morally pure, to relate one's sexual nature to God, and to avoid the sin of violating other persons. It is difficult to see how these motives can be labeled "self-violation."

Others may say that the above interpretation of masturbation is defensive. This criticism is correct. I have defended the thesis that it is possible for a limited amount of male masturbation to occur under certain circumstances and not be a sinful practice. However, in light of this criticism, it is necessary to point out that the materialists defend the general thesis that "no masturbation is sinful" and their opponents defend the general thesis that "all masturbation is sinful." They are both defensive.

Others may say that I have been inconsistent in that I have labeled fantasy during masturbation as being evil but I do not make this distinction concerning dreaming about sexual experiences during nocturnal emissions. This criticism shifts words and meanings. The word "fantasy" is used in relation to masturbation and the word "dreaming" is used in relation to nocturnal emissions. These words do not involve equal mental processes. During fantasy the conscious mind is at work and the person is, therefore, responsible. During dreaming the conscious mind is at rest and the subconscious mind is active. Therefore, the person is not responsible.

An explanation of the mental and physical processes during nocturnal emissions is in order. During seven or eight hours of sleep the bladder fills and presses against the seminal vesicles and the prostate gland. If the external and internal reservoirs are full of semen, this bladder pressure results in automatic sexual stimulation and arousal. The increasing need for emptying the bladder causes the person to move gradually out of sleep where the conscious mind is at rest toward active mental consciousness, that is waking. During this gradual shift from sleep toward waking the mind is in a kind of "twilight zone" in which the subconscious mind is operating. Ideas and thoughts are mixed, confused, and may move swiftly from one idea, experience, or act to another. These jumbled, topsy-turvy, indiscriminate ideas may involve sexual thoughts or activities that would not be tolerated if the conscious mind were directing thought. To assume that a person is responsible for the God-created process of the wandering and meandering of the sub-conscious mind related to nocturnal emissions and that such experience is sinful is utterly ridiculous.

To summarize, in this chapter we have made an honest effort to put God and sex together in the thinking and behavior of growing young men. It is an effort to keep sex and God from being enemies in your thinking and in your lives. You must claim the wonderful God-created blessing of sex for Christianity and for the purposes of God. This must be done through self-control. The normal place for you to start thinking about sex in relationship to God is during your youth. By understanding the holy relationship between God and sex, you should be able to understand why the misuse and abuse of sex is evil. Thus, you will want to control sex and channel it toward fidelity in marriage.

We have said that masturbation in itself is neither good nor evil. A person's purposes, motives, and the results of his behavior are major in determining whether the act is good or evil. When masturbation is used solely as an occasional limited means of sexual self-control until marriage, it is within the Christian understanding of God's plan and purpose in a young man's life.

The practice of masturbation as described above is to be *temporary and limited*. Human beings are all greatly influenced by habit, and habit especially affects those parts of our lives that involve strong drives, such as hunger, thirst, and sex. Like the tide moving silently and slowly, but with overwhelming force, our little habits can gradually, but surely, take control in our lives and enslave us. To avoid becoming a victim of excessive habit requires prayerful, determined effort. *A young man must control, rule, and direct his sexual drive and not allow it to control, rule, and direct him.* Let us suppose, for example, that a young man during the past few months has practiced masturbation for the purpose of self-control on the average of every seven days. It would be good psychology for him to *lean more on nocturnal emissions* and planned sublimation and lengthen the frequency to two weeks or longer. This is simply for self-assurance so he can say to himself, "With God's help, I am not a slave to my sex drive. I am its master. I am controlling myself."

One final word to you young men: You must use an iron will to prove to your sweetheart, beyond a shadow of a doubt, during your social dating, "going steady," and engagement, that your interest in her is not just sexual, but that your interest is in her as a *total person*. After marriage, you must work even harder to convince your wife that your interest in her is not just sexual. She wants you to love and appreciate her as a total person, and rightly so. For a man to do otherwise is unchristian. Multiplied thousands of men have fallen short of this goal.

We men must cease violating persons and their rights. God created us, male and female, in His image. Our personal relationship to God, in humble belief and faith, must be first. Beyond this faith and flowing from this faith, ultimate value resides in persons and not in things or in animals. All persons are of equal worth and value in the plan of God, regardless of sex, color, or nationality. Other persons must never be used as a means to our personal selfish ends.

CHAPTER 10

A HEALTHY SEXUAL IDENTITY FOR YOUNG WOMEN:
A DISTINCTION BETWEEN REPRODUCTION AND
SEXUALITY, AND A STUDY OF FEMALE MASTURBATION

Charm is deceitful, and beauty is vain, but a woman who fears the Lord is to be praised. *(Proverbs 31:30, RSV)*

A virtuous woman is a crown to her husband.
(Proverbs 12:4, KJV)

But because of the temptation to immorality, each man should have his own wife and *each woman her own husband. The husband should give to his wife her conjugal [sexual] rights,* and likewise the wife to her husband. For the wife does not rule over her own body [sexually], but the husband does; likewise *the husband does not rule over his own body [sexually], but the wife does.* Do not refuse one another. . . .
(I Corinthians 7:2-6, RSV—italics added)

It is important for a young woman growing through adolescence toward adult maturity and toward marriage to develop gradually a *healthy sexual identity; that is, she needs to understand and accept the reality, the nature, and the purposes of her sexuality as God created it in her.* This will help her all through the adolescent and later courtship periods not only to understand herself and to develop a healthy *self-confidence,* but it will give her a divinely anchored source of moral wisdom and guidance and a firm, positive source of sexual self-control.

Actually, young women usually have little trouble in achieving sexual self-control. This is especially true when we compare them with young men. The structures of the sexual natures of young men and young women are fantastically alike; yet the manifestation of their sexual needs is different. With a young man, sexuality is something that tends to speak in loud and certain language, calling for expression. For a young woman, sexuality is just as real, but it is something that is buried deep within her being during her early years and is brought to the surface for self-expression only in the proper environment of faith, trust, and love-making (in marriage) and after a rather long and relaxed period of adequate stimulation. Only then does she move into the realm where it is difficult to maintain sexual control. When young women observe the strong, overt manifestation of young men's sexual natures and note how different it appears from their own sex drive, they often falsely conclude that there is something wrong with them sexually, or that they must be undersexed, or that they ought to pretend to display a sexual interest equal to that of the young men. These ideas are not only false, but they create confusion, and they often cause inner frustrations and guilt.

A young woman may react to these false conclusions in one of two extremely different ways. She may adopt an aggressive approach with young men in an effort to prove to herself that she is sexually normal. Or, in her false fear that she is undersexed, she may easily become conditioned against sex and accept dangerous ideas about her sexuality. That is, she may come to believe that sexuality must be rather sinful and that in order to be a good, moral, spiritual person, she must repress sex and reject it as an unnecessary part of her life. Both of these extremes can lead to personal and social frustration and defeat.

The purpose of this chapter is to discuss some biological facts about the sexual structure of women that should help young women to develop a healthy sexual understanding of themselves.

When God created woman (Genesis 1:27) He gave her certain specific biological characteristics. The sexual and reproductive structures of a woman's body are organized into an intricate and elaborate set of tiny, almost infinite details. When we study the details of these structures, the divine purpose of female sexuality becomes clear and definite.

In order to see this evidence, let us distinguish between (1) the female reproductive organs and their functions, and (2) the female sexual organs and their functions. Let us note the major differences. When we examine the facts involved, it is clear that in the purpose and plan of the Creator, the female reproductive system and the female sexual system were to be two separate systems with two separate functions. This idea is similar to biologists' talking in terms of the respiratory system and the digestive system. Although these two systems are definitely related, they may be thought of as two separate systems with two separate functions.

In the past we have thought of the female reproductive and sexual natures as operating together in one completely integrated unit. As a result of this false thinking, the female reproductive system has been greatly abused. Many unwanted children have been brought into existence. Likewise, the female sexual system has been greatly abused in that female sexuality was limited to the point that women did not enjoy the sexual system as God intended when He created woman.

We now present eight sets of biological evidence to show that although the female reproductive and sexual systems are related to each other in the total bodily system, they were actually created by God as two separate systems with two separate functions.

1. The major female reproductive organs are internal organs. They include the *ovaries,* the *fallopian tubes,* the *womb* and the *vagina.* The major female sexual organs,

including the *clitoris,* the *labia majora* (outer lips) and the *labia minora* (inner lips) are external organs. The clitoris is the female sexual trigger that sets off sexual arousal and sexual *orgasms.* The clitoris is fully a sexual organ and actually has no direct relationship to the processes of reproduction. Of course we may think of the vagina as having both a reproductive and a sexual function. However, this should not cause us to overlook the fact that on the side of the female, the external clitoris is biologically the female sexual trigger. This is not meant to overlook the fact that other factors are involved in a woman's sexual arousal in marriage, such as mutual love, trust, tenderness shown by her husband, his kissing her and caressing her body.

2. A married woman does not have to become sexually aroused and experience a sexual orgasm to become pregnant. In the past, hundreds of married women who have never experienced a sexual orgasm have had one or more pregnancies with normal childbirth. Furthermore, modern medical doctors can effect a pregnancy in a woman by the process of artificial insemination. That is, using a small syringe, at the proper time, the doctor can deposit the *semen* of a male donor, who may be the husband or some other person, into the vagina. A pregnancy results. In this procedure, there has been neither sexual arousal nor orgasm on the part of the woman involved. (It should be understood here that this is used as an illustration and does not advocate artificial insemination.)

3. The Creator made woman with definite sexual needs. Her needs under normal life experiences in marriage seem to call for a sexual experience with her husband one, two or more times per week. This varies considerably with different women. In our research involving 151 young married couples, the wives stated on the average that they would like to have sexual intercourse and orgasms with their husbands every 3.2 days. Assuming that this is a valid measurement of the

normal sexual needs of young married women, there is a great difference between the timing of this need and the fact that a pregnancy can occur only once every nine or ten months.

4. Sometimes it is necessary for a woman to have a surgical operation called a hysterectomy. This word comes from the Greek word "hyster" meaning "womb" or "uterus," and from the Greek "tomia" which means "to cut." Thus, a hysterectomy is a surgical operation which completely removes the womb from the body. Of course, this means that the woman can no longer become pregnant. In the past, in approaching these operations many women experienced much worry and anxiety, thinking that the operation would not only stop reproduction, but would bring an end to her sexual desire and need. This idea rested upon the false assumption that reproduction and sexuality operate as a single unit or system in the female body. The uterus is not a sexual organ. It is a reproductive organ. When it is removed by a surgical operation, a woman's sexual capacity will return to normal after a reasonable recovery from this major surgery.

5. During the period of pregnancy a woman's sexual needs continue normally at the same potential level as before the pregnancy, and in some cases, even at an increased rate. In our research, fifteen percent indicated that their sexual desire declined during the pregnancy, seventy percent stated that it remained the same as before the pregnancy, and fifteen percent said that it increased. The fifteen percent in which desire increased may be composed of wives who had considerable fear about becoming pregnant. This fear limited their sexual capacity. Once they became pregnant, their fear disappeared and they relaxed, allowing their sexual capacities to operate more normally. In answering our questionnaire, the wives called this relaxation of fear an increase in sexual interest or capacity. Those who stated in the research that their sex interest declined may have felt

A Healthy Sexual Identity for Young Women

this way partly as the result of certain physical complications, the doctor's instructions not to have sex relations, ideas of rejecting all sexual interest during pregnancy, or for other reasons. The fact is that God created woman so that her sexual interest and need continue during the period of pregnancy.

6. During the four- to six-day menstrual period, the sexual interest of a woman continues as before or after the period. In some cases, the highest sexual interest and need during an entire cycle occur during the menstrual period. Our research indicated twenty-nine percent of the women stated that their degree of sexual desire continued about the same during the entire twenty-eight-day cycle. There was little change, if any. However, seventy-one percent of the women stated that the degree of their sexual intensity changed during the cycle. Of these seventy-one percent of the sample, thirty-two and one-half percent stated that their sexual desire was highest a few days before the menstrual period, while for twenty-two and one-half percent it was highest during the menstrual period. For twenty-four percent it was highest halfway between menstrual periods, which is near the *ovulation* period. These data seem to indicate that there is no particular pattern that all women follow. The time during the total menstrual cycle when a woman's sexual desire has its highest intensity varies greatly from person to person. However, it is necessary to call attention to two facts—1) that generally speaking, all women can have normal sexual experiences during the menstrual cycle, and 2) that twenty-two and one-half percent of the women in our research indicated that their highest sexual interest was during the menstrual period. It is probable that past restrictions against sex relations during the menstrual period caused members of the sample to indicate non-interest in relations during this period. The reader should understand that this discussion is *not* to argue in favor of sexual intercourse during the menstrual period. Rather, it is simply to come

to grips with the fact that God created women so that, in general, their sexual capacity continues during the menstrual period.

7. Our research indicated that fourteen percent of married women *occasionally* become sexually aroused in dreams and experience a sexual orgasm. Although this percentage of the total sample is small, this indicates that in these women, the sexual system was operating independently from the reproductive system.

8. At ages approximately 45 to 50, the menstrual period which has continued regularly since puberty gradually ceases. This ceasing of the menstrual period is called *menopause.* During this time the woman undergoes some rather major glandular and other biological adjustments. Often these adjustments may cause some emotional anxiety for a few months. Since the menstrual period is a reproductive system procedure, many women in the past have had additional anxiety as they approached the ceasing of the menstrual period. They thought menopause would mean the conclusion of their sexual life. This unfortunate anxiety has rested upon the false assumption that the reproductive and sexual natures of women were a single unit. Assuming normal health, the fact is that after the ceasing of the menstrual period, a woman's sexual desire continues at its normal level through the rest of her life. It gradually declines only with the decline of the body in old age. The sexual system continues to operate after the reproductive system has ceased.

When we consider these eight sets of biological facts, *we are forced to conclude that although a woman's reproductive system and her sexual system have some indirect relationships, they are, in fact, two separate systems with two separate functions. This is according to the plan and purpose of the divine Creator.* This conclusion is in harmony with such Bible passages as Genesis 2:24, Proverbs 5:1-23, Matthew 19:4-6, Mark 10:6-9, I Corinthians 7:2-5, and Hebrews 13:4. A careful study of these passages indicates that they are discussing the sexuality of men and women, its morality, its function, and its control. The topic of reproduction is not directly involved in any of these passages. Of course, there are many important Bible passages directly referring to reproduction, such as Genesis 1:28, Ecclesiastes 3:2, and John 16:21, but this present discussion is concerned specifically with "a healthy sexual identity" for women. Since the family and the home are the basic units of our society, these facts and concepts should be taught and discussed openly in each home in the parent-child inter-personal relationships.

For modern young women to understand that the female reproductive system and the sexual system are separate, with separate functions, has several advantages. It helps women to develop a healthier, more meaningful, and more spiritual attitude toward their reproductive and sexual natures. A woman can understand, once and for all, that she is not just a reproductive being, but that she is a total person, created in the image of God. Acceptance of this view tends to improve the personality development and self-confidence of both man and woman. This view should stabilize a marriage by encouraging development of efficient sexuality and by relieving much marital tension, conflict, and guilt feelings. This increases communication and companionship between husband and wife. Since this improves family unity and solidarity, the family should be a healthier environment for growing children.

This two-system approach tends to help married couples to plan parenthood carefully, and should certainly give a psychological lift to couples who cannot have children of their own. It should also make life more meaningful for married couples after the wife has passed the menopause stage in her life.

All of these factors will result in helping to solve some of our major social and cultural problems such as separation, divorce, sexual promiscuity, venereal disease, and children born out of wedlock. If this idea could take root in the cultures of some underdeveloped countries, it should be of social and cultural significance. In India, for example, the culture and religion think rigidly in terms of reproduction and sexuality as being an inseparable unit. This false assumption is a major cause of much of India's social and family problems.

FEMALE MASTURBATION

Since we discussed somewhat in detail the subject of male masturbation, it is logical in discussing a healthy sexual identity for young women to discuss the subject of female masturbation. The subject of masturbation has been discussed rather extensively in recent years in family literature, but the discussion has dealt largely with male masturbation. Some radical writers have discussed female masturbation and have fully recommended it as "healthy," "harmless," and "social." They usually hide behind the cloak of science; yet pulling their self-righteous robes of arrogance about them, they present no scientific evidence that regular female masturbation is healthy, harmless, and social. Since these same writers also recommend fornication, adultery, and homosexuality as being healthy, harmless, and social, it is necessary to question their ideas about female masturbation. In recent years a few writers have discussed the subject of masturbation from the Christian viewpoint, including Henry A. Bowman, O. Hobart Mowerer, William Glasser, John W. Drakeford, M. D. Hugen, and John C. Howell; however, they largely omit the discussion of female masturbation.

There are several facts to keep in mind while reasoning about female masturbation from the Christian viewpoint:

(1) Neither the Old nor the New Testament discusses this subject; therefore, it is necessary to be guided in our thinking by broad basic Christian principles and scientific facts.

(2) The old wives' tales about female masturbation, such as "Girls who masturbate will never bear any children," are all utterly false.

(3) The male and female sexual systems are in many ways identical. As described in Chapter Three, they each include specific sex nerve endings that are involved in sexual arousal procedures. Both men and women have erotic body zones planned by the Creator for the purpose of sexual arousal. The male and female orgasms both involve a sudden rapid reaction, a dynamic upheaval or explosion of the muscular and vascular systems of their bodies that involves intense personal pleasure.

(4) It is Christian for women (and men) to accept their bodies as good: a creation of God. It is normal for them to become educated concerning the nature, purpose, and functions of their bodies.

Feeling that some current research would throw light on the subject of female masturbation, I asked 103 girls enrolled in my sociology classes (in a church-related college in the southeastern part of the United States) twelve questions about masturbation. The girls, who were now well-aquainted with me as a teacher, were asked not to sign their names, and were requested to write their answers in block letters so that their writing could not be identified. Every effort was made to make their personal responses to the questions completely private and unknown to me. The twelve questions and their replies in percentages were as follows:

1. Did your parents ever talk to you in a friendly way about female masturbation and explain that it was not harmful?

        Yes 6%   No 94%

2. Did your parents ever warn you not to masturbate because it was evil?

        Yes 6%   No 94%

3. If your parents have never talked to you about mas-

turbation, do you think they felt that female masturbation was normal or wrong?

Normal 10%   Wrong 90%

4. Have you ever masturbated to orgasm?

Yes 33%   No 67%

5. If you have never masturbated to orgasm, have you ever tried to masturbate to orgasm and did not succeed?

Yes 14%   No 86%

6. If you have masturbated to orgasm, approximately how often have you masturbated during the last two years (before marriage)?

Twice each month   25%   2-4 times per year   19%
Once each month   31%   2-3 times in all   6%
Once every 2-3 mo.   7%   Once in my lifetime   12%

7. Do you think that girls 17 to 21 normally need to masturbate in order to relieve their sex drive and sex tension?

Yes 35%   No 65%

8. If you have masturbated to orgasm or tried to, have you felt guilty about it?

Yes 76%   No 24%

9. If you have not masturbated to orgasm or tried to, have you wanted to but for some reason decided not to?

Yes 14%   No 86%

10. Do you think that it would be good or bad for a girl to masturbate to orgasm a few times just to know by experience that her body is capable of this experience?

Good 43%   Bad 57%

11. Do you think that a girl should wait until marriage and experience her first orgasm with her husband?

Yes 69%   No 31%

12. Do you think a girl can wait until marriage for sexual orgasms without undue sexual, mental and emotional strain?

Yes 75%   No 25%

Some observations concerning the research are in order.

(1) Ninety-four percent of the parents had said nothing to their daughters about masturbation, and the six percent who did talk to them warned them that it was evil. Ninety percent of the girls felt that their parents thought that masturbation was wrong. One girl stated that she felt that "Parents often assume that their children know more about sex than their children really know."

(2) Thirty-three percent of the girls had masturbated to orgasm, and of those who had not, fourteen percent had attempted to do so but did not succeed. Seventy-six percent of those who had masturbated to orgasm had guilt feelings about it.

(3) Sixty-five percent of the sample felt that girls ages 17 to 21 do not normally need to masturbate in order to relieve their sex drive and sex tension. Seventy-five percent felt that girls can wait until marriage for sexual orgasms without undue sexual, mental, and emotional strain, and sixty-nine percent felt that a girl *should wait* to experience her first orgasm with her husband.

FEMALE MASTURBATION: RIGHT OR WRONG?

In discussing whether female masturbation is right or wrong, we must state emphatically that right and wrong are not determined by the practice of the majority or the minority. Since God created women in His image, right and wrong in their lives must be determined by the divine plan of the Creator.

I would *oppose* single young women practicing masturbation before marriage for the following reasons:

(1) The female sex drive does not demand release through masturbation. It is really not a problem for girls to wait until marriage. Our research indicates this is true. Also, it is generally agreed among

authorities that women do not reach their sexual peak until age twenty-eight or twenty-nine.

(2) It is not necessary for a girl to masturbate in order to know whether or not she is normal sexually. She can trust nature for this. Sexual success in marriage does not depend upon premarital experimentation.

(3) Since a young woman does not have a strong sex drive demanding release, masturbation would be using for individual secret pleasure that which God created for social and spiritual purposes in the one-flesh relationship of marriage. The female orgasm is not just a biological procedure; rather, it is a love response and expression to the one loved, the husband.

(4) In this case, masturbation is an over-emphasis on the physical nature of life and generally results in guilt feelings. One girl in the sample said, "Now I wish I had waited until marriage."

(5) Female masturbation is a violation of the spirit of Biblical instructions to youth, including such passages as Romans 13:14, I Corinthians 6:13, Galatians 5:16, Colossians 3:17, I Timothy 4:12, II Timothy 2:22, James 1:15, I John 2:16.

Some readers may ask, "Have you not set up a double standard, advocating a limited program of masturbation for young men as a method of self-control, and then rejecting masturbation for young women?" My reply is "Yes!" However, the question of a double standard needs to be examined carefully before we condemn all double standards as intrinsically evil. We all tend to object to double standards. In the past we have been largely a patriarchal society; that is, men have held the offices, passed the laws, made the social rules, and, in general, authority has resided in them. Unfortunately, many of the laws and social mores set up by men have not rested on substantial Biblical, social, or biological foundations. For example, in the past in our society women were not allowed to vote or have an education. These were arbitrary double standards set up by men. These standards did not respect women as persons nor meet their needs. Gradually both men and women came to see that such standards were biased and detrimental to women and society. Thus, they have been replaced by social change. Women have been given the right to vote and to be educated. These and other similar double standards are to be deplored.

However, it does not follow that all double standards are evil. For example, because of the superior physical strength and the strong sex drive of man on the one hand, and because of the reproductive nature of woman on the other hand, it is necessary to have some laws protecting women from being exploited sexually by men. These laws constitute a double standard. But reason demands that they are necessary and right because they are grounded in the nature of human nature as created by our Creator-God.

In a similar manner, the Creator created men with a strong, continuous sex drive, described in Chapter Nine, the nature of which demands release by ejaculation. Although women have a sexual nature that in many ways is equal to the sexual nature of men, they have little or no problem of sexual control and have no inherent demand for an ejaculation. Therefore, the concept that "a limited pattern of masturbation for men for purposes of self-control might be necessary, while masturbation is not necessary for women" is a double standard that rests upon the inherent natural sexual differences of men and women. This concept does not violate the rights or needs of either men or women. Thus, this point-of-view is an acceptable and rational double standard that is within the general framework of Christian guidelines.

Some readers will ask, "What about men and women who never marry?" This is a large and complex subject and is really outside of our present discussion, "Sexual Understanding Before Marriage"; however, some comments are in order. The plan of the Creator is *marriage,* not singleness. It is understood that there are cases of extreme circumstances, involving the physical and the mental, or both, in which persons should never marry. And it is true that the Bible is sympathetic with people who choose to forego marriage in lieu of efficient Christian service (I Corinthians 7:1, 8). Yet, we must face the fact that the Bible calls for marriage as the rule in man-woman relationships (Genesis 1:27, 28; 2:24, 25; I Corinthians 7:2-5; Ephesians 5:22-25; I Thessalonians 4:1-8, RSV; I Timothy 3:2, 12). The plan of God is marriage. Singleness for religious service is a cultural tradition and not the plan of God.

Judson and Mary Landis describe the disadvantages of singleness as being:

1. Loneliness
2. The problem of creating an efficient social life in a society built around marriage
3. Regret of never having children
4. The need for relatives to provide emotional security through the years
5. The never-ending embarrassment of matchmaking efforts by relatives and friends
6. The lack of an organized and regular sex life[1]

Concerning the problems of older single people, I recommend Dr. M. D. Hugen's book, *The Church's Ministry to the Older Unmarried* (Eerdmans Publishing Company, Grand Rapids, Michigan, 1958).

[1] Landis, 5th Edition, pp. 91-92.

CHAPTER 11

DEALING WITH PAST SEXUAL SINS

Have mercy upon me, O God, according to thy loving-kindness: according unto the multitude of thy tender mercies blot out my transgressions.

Wash me thoroughly from mine iniquity, and cleanse me from my sin.

For I acknowledge my transgressions: and my sin is ever before me.

Against thee, thee only, have I sinned, and done this evil in thy sight: that thou mightest be justified when thou speakest, and be clear when thou judgest.

Purge me with hyssop, and I shall be clean: wash me, and I shall be whiter than snow.

Make me to hear joy and gladness; that the bones which thou hast broken may rejoice.

Hide thy face from my sins, and blot out all mine iniquities.

Create in me a clean heart, O God, and renew a right spirit within me.

Cast me not away from thy presence; and take not thy Holy Spirit from me.

Restore unto me the joy of thy salvation; and uphold me with thy free Spirit.

Then will I teach transgressors thy ways; and sinners shall be converted unto thee.

For thou desirest not sacrifice; else would I give it: thou delightest not in burnt offering.

The sacrifices of God are a broken spirit: a broken and a contrite heart, O God, thou wilt not despise.

(Psalm 51:1-4, 7-13, 16-17)

There are thousands, even millions of people, young and old, who have committed sexual sins in the past and are living under a burden of personal anxiety, misery, and agony over these past sexual sins. In many cases their consciences continually smite them within. They can truthfully say with David, "My sin is ever before me" (Psalm 51:3). Their one interest is to free themselves in some way from this burden, this anxiety, but they do not know what to do or how to proceed to receive forgiveness and release. In many cases their anxiety is increased because their sexual sin is a secret, except for the other person or persons involved, and must be borne by the individual alone.

There are other cases where the individual, after sexual sin, works hard to rationalize, to control, and to ease his conscience. But even though he may succeed in forcing the guilt into his sub-conscious mind, there will be many circumstances that will cause it to surface, to thrust itself boldly into the stream of conscious thought, and periods of guilt feeling and anxiety will plague him.

How does a person go about receiving complete forgiveness and release from past sexual sins? A college student's experience should throw some light on this problem.

John, a college junior, asked me for a private conference. When he came to my office, he carefully closed the door, indicating the serious nature of the problem at hand. He was pale and rather tense, but had control of himself and seemed determined to do something about his problem. He started by saying, "I should have come to see you a long time ago. My problem is . . . well, I am ashamed to tell you about it. I have never told a living soul about this. But I just have to tell somebody." He hesitated, his lips quivered, and tears welled up in his eyes. I interrupted to give him support and to allow him to regain the courage to continue. I assured him that he was not alone in having a personal problem, and that he was doing the right thing to seek help. I explained that whatever he said to me would be kept in the strictest of professional confidence. Then, I sug-

Dealing With Past Sexual Sins

gested that he go ahead and tell me frankly, in simple language, the details of his problem.

In a halting but determined manner, he began. "Two years ago in the summer, when I was nineteen years old, I went to do some work for a family in my hometown. I was to do some general cleaning and repair work in the home. They were good people, I thought. The children were in school during the day, and the father, a salesman, was out of town for a week. His wife directed my work. She visited with me much of the time while I worked. We talked about many subjects. She was complimentary of me and my work and showed me much kindness. She was thirty-four years of age and was an attractive person. On the fourth day, after we were well-acquainted, she tempted me to have sexual relations with her, and I yielded." At this point John was temporarily overcome with emotion.

After he regained control, he continued. "My conscience bothered me so much that night and the next day that I called and made an excuse and did not go back to finish the work. A few months later the family moved from the community. I have never seen her since. I have never told anyone from that day to this, but I still feel very guilty about it. I came back to college the following fall hoping I could lose myself in my school work and forget the incident. But I couldn't. No matter how hard I've tried, I haven't been able to forget. My guilt feelings have grown steadily worse. I have dated some fine girls, and I really want to get married and have a Christian home and family. Now, I am nearly twenty-two years old, but I feel so unworthy of any girl that I cannot date one more than a few times. Then I turn to another one. My grades have been getting lower and lower, and lately I've been extremely discouraged and depressed. I hate to take up your busy time like this, but I just have to get release from my guilt somehow. I thought maybe you could help me."

At this point, John ceased talking and waited for me

to take over. To give him support, I pointed out that the woman involved was much older than he was and that she had been the aggressor; seemingly, she had willfully planned to trap him and was, therefore, because of her age and her motives, responsible for the experience. He quickly replied, "Yes, that is true, but I am responsible too because I gave in to her." I agreed that he could share a part of the responsibility but suggested that we have to measure responsibility by motives. I asked him if he, in any way, had thoughts, plans, or motives in this direction before she tempted him. He replied, "No! Never! But I did give in to her. I was weak. I should have been stronger. I am guilty." Then he described briefly the experience in the Bible when Joseph slipped out of his coat and fled from Potiphar's wife after she tempted him. "I should have been strong as he was."

Realizing that it was necessary to help John come to grips with his own guilt, I suggested that we accept the fact that he shared some of the responsibility for the experience and that we deal directly with his sin and guilt. I asked him to explain to me how the Bible says a Christian should deal with his sins. He quickly described repentance and confession. I interrupted, "John, it is obvious that you are very, very sorry for your part in this experience. Doesn't this constitute repentance on your part?"

He said, "If I knew how to repent any better, I would have done so a long time ago."

I continued, "Have you ever asked God to forgive you for this sin?"

He quickly said, "Yes, many, many times!"

"Then," I said, "doesn't it follow that God always forgives those who repent and ask for forgiveness?"

"Yes," he said, "but I have not been able to get any release at all. When I try to stop feeling guilty, I seem to be up against a stone wall."

At this point, I attempted to summarize his feelings

and show him that he had not succeeded in accepting God's forgiveness. He agreed on this. I went on to explain that when a person repents and asks for forgiveness, God completely forgives him immediately. Then we looked at some Scriptures describing the nature of God's forgiveness. We read, "As far as the east is from the west, so far does he remove our transgressions from us" (Psalm 103:12, RSV). "John," I asked, "how far is the East from the West?" Without waiting for an answer, I pointed out that each is an infinite distance from the other. "And this," I said, "is simply a picture of how God removes our sins when we repent and ask for forgiveness."

Then we read from Micah 7:19, another illustration of God's complete forgiveness. "He (God) will have compassion upon us ... thou (He) wilt cast all their sins into the depths of the sea." I mentioned that in some places the ocean is deeper than the mountains are high. Those things that are cast to the bottom of the ocean are left there permanently. By this time, John was quiet and listening intently, literally hanging on every word. We continued, looking at another familiar passage, "Come now, and let us reason together, saith the Lord; though your sins be as scarlet, they shall be as white as snow" (Isaiah 1:18). I explained that the color scarlet, or the brightest color, is used often in the Scriptures to describe extreme sin. In contrast, the whiteness of fresh snow is used to describe the condition of God's complete forgiveness of sin. The picture here is that when God forgives us of sin, the forgiveness is as complete as the change from crimson red to the whiteness of snow.

We read one other passage in which the prophet Jeremiah quoted the Lord God, "I will forgive their iniquity, and I will remember their sin no more" (Jeremiah 31:34). John saw that the context of this verse, and the rest of these Scripture passages, was saying literally that God not only forgives our sins completely, but He never remembers them again.

I suggested to John that we now apply these illustrations of divine forgiveness to his problems. I repeated them. "The Lord removes our sins an infinite distance away from us—as far as East is from West, and as far as it is to the bottom of the ocean. God changes our guilt from crimson red to the whiteness of new snow. He forgets our sins forever. Even these pictures are feeble descriptions of the reality of God's true forgiveness. Now, John, in looking at your situation, we can say that you have definitely sinned. And we can say, secondly, that you have thoroughly repented. Also, you have petitioned God for His forgiveness. Now, God *has* forgiven you as fully and completely as these pictures describe. In other words, it is a fact that you are now completely forgiven. You must accept this fact, respond to it, and live by it. John, this really means that *in the sight of God, you are now as if you had never had this experience* with this woman."

I paused and inquired, "Have you followed me?"

"Yes," he replied, "this helps a lot." In finishing the conversation that day, we discussed the completeness of God's forgiveness that fits into God's plan of infinite love and grace for all of us.

"Before you go," I said, "I want to suggest that you never tell this experience to another person as long as you live. The only possible exception would be that, previous to your marriage, you might tell your prospective marriage partner. It was right for you to tell me as a private counselor, but since your forgiveness is complete there is no reason ever to tell anyone else. If, in the future, you are tempted to feel guilty, remember these four Bible pictures we have described today. Remember that in God's sight, you are as if you had never done this thing. So, in the future, live, feel, and act as if it had never happened. As you finish your college work, continue the normal processes of courtship. Select the girl of your choice. You are worthy of her love and devotion. Move into the occupation of your choice as God leads you. And, of course, since God has done so much for you, you will want to put Him first in your life and love and serve Him."

John said, "You don't have to worry about that!" He paused, a flood of emotion crossed his face, and then he made this significant statement: "The road a person must travel to get back to the Lord after he has sinned is too hard for him to have to travel it very often." Presently, John stood up to leave. He said, "I haven't felt like this in two years." Gripping and pumping my hand, he thanked me over and over again as he left. It was three days before our paths crossed again. This time he wore a smile, and we exchanged a friendly greeting in passing. During the days until he graduated, I saw John many times. He always went out of his way to speak and to be kind. He always appeared happy, but never did he discuss or refer to the matter again . . . nor did I.

Let us note the processes involved in John's experience:

1. He admitted to himself that he had sinned (Psalm 51:3).

2. He possessed genuine regret, sorrow, and contrition for his sin (Psalm 51:9).

3. He realized that he could not solve his problem alone (Psalm 51:16).

4. In his inner distress and guilt feelings, he was anxiously seeking forgiveness and pardon (Psalm 51:9).

5. He prayed and asked God to forgive him (Psalm 51:1, 7, 10).

6. When he could not understand or accept God's free forgiveness, he sought out a counselor to help him. He trustingly shared in confidence the details of his problem, anxious to receive help (Proverbs 12:15).

7. When the nature of God's forgiveness, through the study of the Scriptures, was made clear and simple to him, he was able to accept God's personal for-

giveness. Thus he received and welcomed total joyful release (Psalm 51:8).

8. The experience drew him spiritually near to God, and he used it as a wall, a dike, to protect him from further sexual sin (Psalm 51:12-13). Thus John went his way in life determined to follow the instructions of Jesus, "Go, and sin no more" (John 8:11).

It is obvious that John made two mistakes in handling his problem. First, he *waited too long* to seek help. He could have been spared many months of anguish had he sought help earlier. People should feel free to talk to their pastor or a Christian counselor, psychologist, nurse, doctor, a trusted Sunday school teacher or friend who is qualified to give spiritual help.

Second, John seemed to have the *false idea that sexual sins are more evil, immoral, and ungodly that any other sin.*

It is easy to understand why many people make this mistake. Four reasons appear which may help explain it.

1. Another person has been violated.
2. The social implications involved are major.
3. Sex is a broad, deep, drive that is related to total life.
4. The more highly developed and mature a person's Christian ideals and values, the more intensely he suffers from guilt feelings.

But this reasoning is looking at sin from the human point of view and overlooks the teachings of the Scriptures on the nature of God, sin, and forgiveness. When a person seeks forgiveness, what stands in the way of God's willingness to forgive any sin is basically an attitude of unbelief and rebellion toward God on the part of the sinner. It is this *unbelief and rebellion that causes specific acts* such as the abuse of sex, telling a lie, cheating on an examination, or stealing. Both the inner rebellion and the fruit of the rebellion, the specific act committed by a person, are evil in the sight of God. But

Dealing With Past Sexual Sins

the Scriptures teach that no one specific human act is really any more sinful than any other specific act.[1] A sexual sin, telling a lie, cheating on an examination, or stealing are all alike in the sight of God and are all fully and equally forgiven when the person committing the sin repents and asks God for forgiveness.

To help deal efficiently with past sexual sins, it is well for us to discuss more fully some Biblical ideas about the nature of men and women, sin, and forgiveness.[2] The central core of Bible teaching is that our infinite, eternal God created both man and woman in His image (Genesis 1:27). Being created in the image of God means, among other things, that we live in a world of ideas, that we are creatures of feelings, motives, attitudes, aspirations, and values. It means that we are endowed with freedom of choice. The sacredness of the personality of both men and women is evident by the fact that we are created in God's image and by the fact that Christ died for us. Since we were created in the image of God, every person possesses dignity and is worthy of personal respect and Christian love, regardless of color, race, creed, or culture.

Because we men and women were created free to choose between right and wrong, we are capable of sin. Sin is an inward condition of the heart that causes us to rebel against God our Creator, against His plan and His will for our lives. It causes us to make bad choices. When we sin and rebel against God, we develop guilt feelings and our conscience smites us. Conscience is the personal inner acceptance and internalizing of the spiritual and moral teachings and standards of our family and community as being right and necessary for our

[1] Readers concerned about this point should study thoroughly the following Bible passages: Nehemiah 9:17; Psalms 85:2, 86:5, 103:3, 107:19; Isaiah 55:7; Jeremiah 33:8; John 2:32, 3:16; Philippians 4:19; Hebrews 11:6; I Peter 5:7; II Peter 3:9; and Revelation 22:17.

[2] This description of the nature of man, sin, and forgiveness is based on the "Baptist Faith and Message" adopted by the Southern Baptist Convention in Kansas City, Missouri, May 9, 1963.

own conduct and character. It normally produces a feeling of guilt and shame when we violate or are tempted to violate right conduct. Conscience is inherent in the social and psychological nature of human nature. However, it can be trained in evil directions.

Salvation from sin involves two inseparable ideas: (1) repentance and (2) faith. Repentance means "change of mind." It involves genuine sorrow for our sins and an actual turning away from all our sins. When a non-Christian turns away from his sins in genuine repentance, he turns to God and in "faith" accepts Christ as his personal Lord and Savior, committing his total personality and life to Him. Faith is complete acceptance of, total, absolute commitment to, and confident dependence on Christ. Faith includes knowledge, but it goes beyond knowledge. It is God's Holy Spirit who leads the non-Christian to repent and to exercise faith in Christ. Yet, the non-Christian is not passive in this process. God respects the freedom of man, and man is freely active in the processes of repentance and faith. Repentance and faith are experiences of God's mercy and grace and are often called "Regeneration" or the "New Birth." Persons who have received Christ through repentance and faith are called believers or Christians. Thus, a non-Christian in receiving salvation in Christ is forgiven of all sins, including all sexual sins. In the sight of God, it is as if he had never committed these past sins.

However, believers, having freedom of choice, may fall into sin through neglect and temptation. They may commit many types of sin, including sexual sins. When one sins, he grieves the Holy Spirit and becomes a stumbling block to the cause of Christ and His Gospel. But a believer who has sinned, when led of the Holy Spirit, can repent of his sin, confess his sin directly to God, and ask for forgiveness. His sin is then fully forgiven.

God, by His very nature, loves those created in His image—all men and women. When we repent of our sins, God always deals with us in love and mercy. His complete forgiveness is the result of His grace. The word "grace" is a beautiful word because it refers to the total, outgoing nature of God. It describes His sovereign goodness, His infinite wisdom, His perfect holiness, and His loving-kindness toward repenting sinners. It is God's grace that causes Him to give us the undeserved favor of complete forgiveness of all our sins—including our sexual sins. It is God's grace that causes Him to forget our sins forever.

CHAPTER 12

SOME PRACTICAL CHRISTIAN GUIDELINES FOR SEXUAL CONTROL FROM PUBERTY UNTIL MARRIAGE

In all thy ways [guidelines and interpersonal social situations] acknowledge him, and he shall direct thy paths.

(Proverbs 3:6, KJV)

Finally, brethren, whatsoever things are true, whatsoever things are honest, whatsoever things are just, whatsoever things are pure; whatsoever things are lovely, whatsoever things are of good report; if there be any virtue, and if there be any praise, think on these things [guidelines]. *(Philippians 4:8, KJV)*

This final chapter is an effort to summarize the ideas and principles set forth in the first eleven chapters to assist you young people in working out some basic guidelines for your own lives. In Chapter Eight we suggested that engaged couples work out together a life philosophy that they would use to guide them both in planning and living out their lives together in marriage. The following guidelines are designed to be of help to couples in such planning. I suggest that couples dating seriously or engaged plan a date where they can carefully read and discuss these guidelines together. It should help them to clarify and refine their own ideas and ideals and help them to understand each other's ideas and ideals. This type of dialogue should be a healthy, interpersonal experience for serious thinking young lovers. (Or, these guidelines could be used as a launching pad for youth group discussions.)

Christians believe in God as the infinite, eternal Creator of the universe and all life. This is the core idea of Christianity. It may be that the most profound and most significant words in the Bible are the words, "In the beginning God created . . ." (Genesis 1:1). We Christians believe that God existed before the universe and life. God is personal, self-sufficient, free, intelligent, moral, and sovereign. He is infinite in all qualities. He created the universe and all life (Genesis 1:1; Colossians 1:16; Hebrews 11:3). God did not make the world out of some pre-existent "stuff," nor did He make it out of Himself. He created that which did not exist.

The method used in creation is not explained in the Bible. It is simply stated and assumed. God's creation is the result of intelligent purpose. The different parts of the whole are related to one another. It is marked by order, continuity, reproductivity, law, and unity.

In general, the Christian concept of creation is that the universe came from God. The "person," the "mind," and the "will" of God are the sole cause and explanation of creation. God existed first. Not only did He bring the physical and human world into existence, but the world continues to depend on Him. Christians carefully avoid theories that would identify God with nature or beliefs that He created the world and withdrew, having nothing to do with it any longer.

Since so many persons today openly challenge the concept of belief in God, it may be well to digress briefly to state the rational basis for belief in God.

First you must come to grips with the truth that all persons have a set of beliefs and values which direct their interpretations of facts, of life. Christians have never been ashamed of their assumption that God created the universe. They proudly state it publicly. One should suspect any professor (or anyone else) who refuses to admit his assumptions about life or who avoids stating them openly, in simple language. It is obvious that he is at-

Sexual Understanding Before Marriage

tempting to sneak ideas in the "back door" of the student's mind which he does not have the courage to bring to the "front door."

What is the alternative to belief in God? It would have to be some type of "atheism." In any effort to explain the universe, theist or atheist *must assume something as a starting point.* The Bible assumes God. People who deny God must assume something else in the beginning. We must admit that problems are involved in assuming that in the beginning there existed either an infinite God or only simple forms of life. We can always ask, "Where did God or these simple forms come from?" If we assume God, we may ask, how did "mind" create "matter"? If we assume simple forms of physical life without God, we may ask, how did "matter" create "mind"?

When we get past these original problems, the assumption of an infinite God is rational and the atheistic assumption is irrational. The thinking Christian asks the person denying God: How did matter (assumed) get around to being organized? to moving? to living? to thinking? to being moral? to being personal?

Each level of change and progress involves incredible problems. Can we say that organized matter and life came out of chaos? that movement came out of the static? that living things came out of the non-living? that thinking came out of the non-thinking? that morals came out of the non-moral? that the personal came out of the impersonal? This is irrational. It is nonsense. On the other hand, it is rational to say that this universe came into existence through the handiwork of an infinite, personal God who created matter, organized it, and endowed it with movement, life, mind, morals, and personality. This is the Christian viewpoint. Since the infinitely organized universe and life are here, now, it follows that an infinite personal God has to be. No other explanation of the origin of the universe and life is rational or intelligent.

Often the skeptic says, "Since scientists can now create life, does this not destroy the idea of God?" The skeptic is using the word "create" dishonestly. Actually, scientists never create anything. They simply experiment with the materials and processes God created. Therefore, instead of creating life, scientists have simply *copied* God's method of creating life. They use the chemical elements and their properties and processes that God created in the beginning to form life. Man's ability to copy God's methods has nothing to do with the existence of God. Those people who talk in beautiful language about "nature" and the "laws of nature" are really talking about God and the laws of nature that God created.

Thus our Judeo-Christian basic guideline is the existence of God. He is a person, an infinite person, whereas we are finite persons. He exists outside and above us, yet He created us and is concerned about us; He cares for us and works in and through us. He exists outside and above the family, the community, the nations and their history, yet He works in and through the family, the community, the nations, and history.

GUIDELINE 2

Christians believe that man and woman were created in the image of God. Probably the second most significant Bible passage is, "So God created man in his own image, in the image of God created he him; male and female created he them" (Genesis 1:27). This same idea is taught by Paul (Colossians 3:9, 10) and James (James 3:8, 9) in the New Testament. Thus we are saying that:

> God created each man and each woman a soul, a self, a unit, an agent, a person composed of mind (spiritual, mental, emotional, social, moral). At the same time, He created them with fleshly bodies (physical, reproductive, sexual). . . . The sacredness of human personality is evident, in that God created man in His own image and in that Christ died for man. Therefore, the idea that value resides in persons, and not in animals or things, is inherent in the creative mind of God. This means that

every man and woman possesses dignity, worth, and value.[1]

GUIDELINE 3

Christians believe that all persons being created in the image of God are, therefore, active knowing agents, selves, or souls. Being free to act, the behavior of each person is determined by his own personal *motives* and *intentions.* He is aware of his intentions and motives; they are directed toward his particular *goals.* His motives and goals are *meaningful* to him.

Each individual finds himself in many different types of social situations. In every social situation a person can *choose* between many possible ways of behavior. Each individual is free (within limits) to select his method of behavior in every social situation. The social situation does not and should not control the individual's behavior. A Christian should not respond mechanically to every social situation. He should conduct himself in terms of the meanings of his Christian guidelines. In other words, he is free to do right. However, it is also true that every person in many social situations is free to behave in keeping with the social situation, whether the situation is good or bad. It is realistic to say that all of us are greatly influenced by the behavior of social groups, especially our peer group.

This guideline refers to the freedom we all have in choosing our patterns of conduct. We are free to do *good* or *evil.* The sinful nature of men and women leads many, young and old, to follow the crowd and to choose evil in social situations. Often sin takes over in a person's life, and he cannot tell right from wrong. The strength and depth of the sinful depravity of human beings is a stern reality that must not be overlooked by youth in selecting guidelines for life. An individual in his room alone may follow consistent moral ideals. Yet the same individual in a social situation of peers may

[1] Miles, *Sexual Happiness in Marriage*, p. 36.

Some Practical Christian Guidelines for Sexual Control From Puberty Until Marriage

193

make evil decisions. This is the result of sinful pride, self-centeredness, and vanity. Our sinful nature may cause us to choose popularity instead of righteousness, property instead of persons, hate instead of love, and self-gratification instead of self-control.

The wonderful blessing of the freedom of choice carries with it the responsibility of choosing between right and wrong. In the light of man's sinful nature, this is an awesome responsibility. We need divine leadership to help us make right decisions in all social situations. In all social situations a Christian must distinguish between Christian values and social customs. We must view life in terms of optimism and hope and not in terms of pessimism and despair. We must view life in terms of the dimension of eternity. In making choices we must remember that man, his mind, and his spirit are indestructible. We must view the core of life and the universe as being basically spiritual.

Yes, our social situations tend to influence our behavior. Christians live in the world of social situations, but must not follow the conduct of social situations that violate our Christian nature and our Christian guidelines.

GUIDELINE 4

Christians believe that the human family is the basic organized unit upon which all human, social, and cultural development rests. A third most significant and beautiful Bible passage is, "Therefore shall a man leave his father and his mother, and shall cleave unto his wife: and they shall be one flesh" (Genesis 2:24). The God-created human family (father, mother, son, and daughter) is the cradle of human personality and security. The family is the seedbed of basic human values and human progress. It is the citadel of civilization; it is the social foundation of the kingdom of God.

GUIDELINE 5

Christians believe that human sexuality is one of the

strongest social forces in existence. When human sexuality is harnessed, guided, and used in marriage according to the plan of God our Creator, it is good and becomes one of the greatest blessings in the process of human experience. In a national, church-related, family life conference Dr. Herbert R. Howard stated in the opening address that "Marriage is first, last, and always a sex relationship."[2] By this statement, he was not saying that sex is *the* most important relationship in marriage. Rather he was saying that in marriage sex is a relationship

(1) that is always present,
(2) that must always be reckoned with,
(3) that must always be accounted for, and
(4) in which husbands' and wives' sexual needs must always be met.

GUIDELINE 6

Christians believe that all persons should recognize authority outside of themselves and submit humbly and cooperatively to it. I refer to the authority of God, the Bible, the family, the laws of nature, the national Constitution, and the state and community authorities. Rules and regulations are inherent in the nature of life. It is impossible to have a normal life without submission to and following of some authority outside of us as individuals. Contrary to the thinking of some who ought to know better, obeying an authority outside of us does not limit our freedom, but rather it gives us freedom. It makes freedom, growth, and maturity possible.

GUIDELINE 7

Christians believe that premarital sexual intercourse is a direct violation of the person and purpose of God. It is a direct violation of the spirit and the letter of the Bible. Appendix I is a formal discussion of this topic.

[2] Herbert R. Howard, *The Church and the Christian Family,* Family Life Department, Baptist Sunday School Board, 1963, p. 12xiv.

GUIDELINE 8

Christians believe that premarital sexual intercourse blocks normal personality development and self-realization. The inner system of reality of the fornicator which is characterized by egocentric, selfish motives blocks

(1) fellowship with God,
(2) the ability to love,
(3) the ability to complete self-surrender,
(4) the ability to complete self-giving, and
(5) spiritual, moral, emotional, social, and intellectual growth.

GUIDELINE 9

Christians believe that premarital sexual intercourse violates other persons, even if they consent to the experience. Wherever there is an offender, there is a victim. The Bible teaches that "we are our brother's keeper and protector." This is true because in the created world ultimate values reside in persons who are created in the image of God—not in animals or things. Persons created in the image of God are of infinite worth and value in the world of social and interpersonal relationships. All persons are valuable regardless of race, color, creed, or culture. In the sight of God, all persons have equal worth and value in the created plan of the systems in which we live. Persons created in the image of God should never be used by a Christian nor anyone else as a means to personal selfish ends. Thus, premarital sexual intercourse has to be rejected.

GUIDELINE 10

Christians believe that premarital sexual intercourse gradually destroys the basic foundation stones upon which the superstructure of effective family life rests. When God created man and woman in His image and gave them the capacity to reproduce, and gave them both sexuality, He created the family. God's creative plan for the family includes specific plans

(1) for husband-wife relationships,
(2) for parent-child relationships,
(3) for family-community relationships,
(4) for economic and government organization, and
(5) for religious and moral progress, including evangelism and missions.

These plans are easily identified through divine revelation and through scientific studies of human nature on the level of biology, psychology, and sociology.

GUIDELINE 11

Finally, *Christians believe that it is impossible for a mature, intelligent person logically to believe in and defend premarital sexual intercourse.* To believe logically in premarital sexual intercourse, a man must defend the right of any man to have had sexual intercourse with his mother before she was married. He must defend the right of any man to have sexual intercourse with his sister before she is married. He must defend the right of any man to have had sexual intercourse with his wife before he married her. He must defend the right of any man to have sexual intercourse with his daughter before she is married. Few civilized persons could really believe and accept this. It is intelligent and Christian for a man to treat other women as he would have other men treat his mother, his sisters, his wife and his daughters.

I am certain that every youth who has read this far has solid plans, hopes, and dreams for a good life, a full life of personal fulfillment and service to others. Your thoughts and your emotions throb with ardent desire to attain the maximum purposes and goals in your life. *Your ambitions can be realized.* As you contemplate the above guidelines and plan to realize your life ambitions, be sure to fuse Christianity, marriage, sexuality, and education in your life as you look to the future. A successful life calls for labor united with play, rest, and sleep. Spend some time alone reading and in prayer and meditation, yet be an extrovert in social relationships with your family and friends. Saturate your mind with the Word of God, the will of God, and the leadership of the Holy Spirit. Choose values that are consistent. Remember that REPENTANCE OF SIN, AND COMPLETE SURRENDER TO CHRIST, plus

Inwardly
1. Self-knowledge
2. Self-respect
3. Self-denial and
4. Self-control, plus

Outwardly, respect and concern for the
1. Needs
2. Rights
3. Dignity and
4. Self-autonomy of all persons, plus

Methods of procedure, including
1. Sincerity and humility
2. Systematic organization
3. Singular punctuality and
4. Old-fashioned happy hard work:

These alone lead to
1. SPIRITUAL GROWTH
2. PERSONAL SECURITY
3. SOCIAL BALANCE and the
4. FULLNESS OF ETERNAL LIFE.

Do not be afraid of truth or reality. Move along with changing culture as long as the community habits do not violate universal values that rest upon natural, moral, and divine law. Continue to adjust and readjust yourself to the fact that time moves on.

But remember, to have a happy marriage and a fruitful life, your personal character and conduct must be moral. It must conform to God's purpose for human life. Be sensitive to the line between right and wrong. Where you are on the road is not as important as the direction in which you are headed. It is important for you to live a life of consistent moral conduct and behavior *now* in these vital and important years of your life.

APPENDIX I

The Biblical Case for Premarital Chastity

The evidences that call for the rejection of premarital sex relations are logically divided into (1) Biblical evidences and (2) social and psychological evidences. The social and psychological evidences have been presented in Chapter Four. This appendix will attempt a formal examination of the Biblical evidences. Modern youth are asking some pertinent questions about the Bible and sex. (1) What is the Biblical point of view about premarital sex relations and the misuse and abuse of sex? (2) What does the Bible have to say about our attitudes and behavior as related to sex from puberty to marriage? (3) Does the Bible shed enough light on this subject to give us solid principles to follow? (4) Or as some seem to say, is the matter of sex a rather irrelevant matter to be left entirely to the individual?

An examination of the Scriptures in light of these questions is long overdue. We will attempt to examine (1) Bible words which describe sexual abuse, (2) Jesus' concept of the nature of sin as related to sex, (3) the Biblical meaning of the word "fornication," (4) some Biblical moral exhortations to youth, and (5) the Biblical concept of the knowledge imparted through sexual intercourse.

This entire discussion should be understood in light of the positive plan and purpose of God in creating sex, as discussed in the twelve earlier chapters.

Bible Words Describing Sexual Abuse

The Bible encourages young people to follow a life of strict self-control, including sexual control. In general, the Scriptures teach that any person who has sexual intercourse outside of marriage has committed sin against God and against the plan of God for human sexuality. Such words as adultery, fornication, immorality, uncleanness, licentiousness, and lust are used to describe sexual sins. It is helpful for us to understand the Biblical use of these words to get a clear picture of Christian teaching about sex.

The word "fornication" (porneia) basically refers to all sexual immorality in general or to voluntary sexual intercourse between an unmarried person and another person of the opposite sex. This word is often translated "immorality." The word fornication will be discussed in detail, presently. The word "adultery" basically refers to voluntary sexual intercourse between a married man or woman with any person other than his lawful wife or her lawful husband (Exodus 20:14; Mark 10:19; Romans 13:9). It also refers to the *relationship* in which such a couple becomes involved. Sexual abuse is often associated with the word "uncleanness" (Romans 6:12; II Corinthians 1:21; Galatians 5:19; Ephesians 5:3; Colossians 3:5). The word "licentiousness" refers to the behavior of persons who habitually practice sexual looseness (Galatians 5:19, RSV).

Some lists of sins in the New Testament place sexual abuse beside other sins such as idolatry, hatred, envy, murder, and drunkenness (I Corinthians 6:9; Galatians 5:19-22). These passages seem to assume that the nature of sexual abuse is equivalent to the evil nature of hate, drunkenness, idolatry, and murder.

Conversation About Sex

The Scriptures seem to be so concerned about sexual control that we are warned about the proper use of sex in conversation. Paul urges the Colossians to "once and

for all put aside . . . abusive filthy talk from your lips"
(Colossians 3:8). In discussing immorality with the Christians at Ephesus, Paul says, "Stop using foul language about sex (Ephesians 4:29). Let there be no more filthiness, silly talk, or laughter about sex. It is crude and unbecoming to Christians (5:4). When talking about sex use dignified language suitable for the occasion, which God can use to help those who are listening (4:29). Always be thankful for the blessing of sex (5:4)" (a free translation based on Williams and Phillips). It is well to note that the assumption that Christians should never talk about sex is utterly false. The writers of both the Old and New Testament talked frankly and somewhat in detail about human sexual relationships, yet with dignity and without offense (Proverbs 5:1-23; Song of Solomon; I Corinthians 7:1-5).

The Nature of Sin

When one understands the New Testament view of the basic nature of sin, it will help in understanding New Testament ideas about the nature of sexual sin. To the Pharisees sin was an external act, such as eating certain food, washing one's hands or plate improperly, and other formal rituals. To counteract this false teaching Jesus described sin as an inward condition of a person's heart. He said to the multitude, "Listen, and understand this thoroughly! It is not what goes into a man's mouth that makes him common or unclean (Matthew 15:11). . . . But the things that come out of a man's mouth come from his heart and mind, and it is they that really make a man unclean. For it is from a man's mind that evil thoughts arise — murder, adultery, lust, theft, perjury, and blasphemy" (Matthew 15:18, 19, *Phillips* translation).

The source of sin, the real cause of sin, according to Jesus, is the inner attitudes, feelings, and motives of the mind and heart. The mind and heart are the central fountain of human life. Our thoughts, ideas, words, acts, and behavior are the streams that flow from that central fountain. Sin is an attitude of the mind and heart that violates the purpose and will of God. Therefore, sexual sin is an attitude of the mind and heart that violates the purpose and will of God for sex. This is illustrated when Jesus said in the Sermon on the Mount, "Whosoever looketh on a woman to lust after her has committed adultery with her already in his heart." Thus, sexual sin is an inward attitude and condition of the mind and heart.

The Relation of Motives to Acts

Modern Christian young people need to develop a proper understanding concerning the relation of inner attitudes, thoughts, and motives to outer words and acts. Some people seem to imply that our external acts are insignificant and unimportant. This implication is false and dangerous. Our inner thoughts and motives and our external words and acts are both a part of us. It is a sin for a man to wish in his heart that he could have sexual intercourse with his neighbor's wife. It would obviously be a greater sin if he would put his wish into external actuality, since this would involve another person. As stated in Chapter Seven, those modern thinkers who try to ignore the significance of external acts are as much out of line with the ideas of Jesus as the Pharisees who tried to ignore the significance of the inner motives. Jesus, in His emphasis on inner motives, was trying to correct the false ideas of the Pharisees. He did not intend to teach that external acts are insignificant. This is illustrated in His attitude toward the woman taken in adultery. He not only forgave her but said, "Go, and sin no more" (John 8:11). Thus, He was rejecting the external act as evil.

Let us digress to point out that since sin is an inward condition of the heart, it is understandable why Jesus and the apostles kept calling for repentance and a new birth, that is, a change of the inner attitudes and motives of the mind and heart toward God, His plan and purpose.

Does the Bible Discuss Premarital Sex Relations?

Let us examine the idea of those people who say the Bible does not discuss premarital sex relations and who assume, by implication, that Christianity has no Scriptural foundations for objecting to premarital sex relations. For example, one author writes, "The New Testament is in some respects even less helpful than the Old if one is looking for direct reference to premarital sex relations and specific advice on the problems thereof."[1]

This kind of interpretation has furnished rationalization for many people who are not familiar with the Scriptures. It is an exceedingly questionable position and calls for a thorough examination of all the facts involved.

1. In the first place, the argument rests upon the assumed silence of the Scriptures. This is poor Bible interpretation and is a rather shaky foundation for such a major conclusion. It is like saying that since the Bible does not have "direct reference" to stealing airplanes or television sets, and "does not give specific advice on the problems thereof," there is really no Biblical foundation for objecting to stealing airplanes and television sets.

During New Testament days, since marriage followed soon after puberty, it is obvious that the problem of premarital sexual intercourse was not as big a problem as it is in our advanced culture where a long period of education is normal and where a larger percentage of young people, ages fifteen to twenty-five, are unmarried. Thus, the New Testament writers would not say as much about premarital sex relations as they would about adultery, since most Hebrew adults were married.

2. The assumption seems to be blind to the broad Biblical attitude that (1) positively, sex was created for

[1] William Graham Cole, *Sex and Love in the Bible*, Association Press, p. 247.

marriage and belongs only to marriage, and (2) negatively, the Bible condemns all immorality whether in thought, word, or act, whether one is a youth or an adult, single or married, as being a violation of the plan and will of God and as characteristic of those people who are outside of the kingdom of God.

3. We can assume that the basic message of the Gospel concerning sin, salvation, and the Christian life applies as fully to single people from puberty to marriage as it does to married adults.

4. How do we explain the meaning of the word "fornication" (Greek, *porneia*) as defined above? It is evident that the meaning of fornication as used in the New Testament varies. Baker's *Dictionary of Theology* (1960) defines fornication as follows: "In its more restricted sense fornication denotes voluntary sexual communion between an unmarried person and one of the opposite sex. In a wider sense, *porneia* signifies unlawful cohabitation of either sex with a married person. In its widest sense *porneia* denotes immorality in general, as every kind of sexual transgression." Note that unmarried people are included in all of the shades of meaning.

Webster's Third New International Dictionary (unabridged 1961) defines fornication as "human sexual intercourse other than between a man and his wife: sexual intercourse between a spouse and an unmarried person; sexual intercourse between unmarried people; sexual intercourse on the part of an unmarried person accomplished with consent and not deemed adultery."

Some form of the word fornication (*porneia, porneue, ekporneuo, and pornos*) appears thirty-nine times in the New Testament. After a study of the context of these passages in light of the above definitions, we may conclude that fornication has three different meanings as used in the New Testament.

1. In some passages, fornication refers to all sexual immorality in general (John 8:41; Acts 15:20, 29; 21:25; Romans 1:29; I Corinthians 5:1; 6:13, 18; II Corinthians

12:21; Ephesians 5:3). However, it is necessary to point out that all these passages include the concept of voluntary sexual intercourse of a single person with a married person or a single person with another single person. Many of these passages include the concept of prostitution (i.e. a woman rendering sexual favors to a man for pay). Note that when fornication refers to prostitution, this does not rule out single people.

2. In two passages, the word fornication is used as a synonym for the word adultery (Matthew 5:32 and 19:9).

3. In four passages, the words adultery and fornication are both used, indicating a definite distinction between the two words (Matthew 15:19; Mark 7:21; I Corinthians 6:9; and Galatians 5:19). Since adultery only includes the behavior of married people, the word fornication would have to mean (among other things) sexual intercourse and other sexual abuses of single people. *This is a direct reference to premarital relations.*

4. In two passages, fornication refers to voluntary sexual intercourse between unmarried people or between an unmarried person and a married person. In discussing whether or not single people should marry, Paul said to the Corinthians, "to avoid fornication [i.e. premarital sexual intercourse] let every man have his own wife, and let every woman have her own husband" (I Corinthians 7:2, RSV). In discussing the importance of a clean moral life, Paul wrote to the Christians in Thessalonica, "For this is the will of God, your sanctification: that you abstain from immorality [i.e. premarital sex relations]; that each one of you know how to take a wife for himself in holiness and honor, not in the passion of lust like heathen who do not know God" (I Thessalonians 4:3-5, RSV). In both passages Paul is warning unmarried people about the temptation to immorality (fornication). In both cases, Paul advocated marriage as an antidote to a single life of immorality (i.e. premarital sex relations). In both cases, *it is clear, beyond possible doubt, that Paul was specifically objecting to premarital sexual intercourse.*

We may summarize the New Testament use of the word fornication *(porneia)* as follows:

1. Out of thirty-nine passages, thirty-seven of them include the concept of premarital sexual intercourse as being opposed to the plan and will of God. The only exceptions are the two passages using fornication as a synonym for adultery.

2. Four passages distinguish between fornication and adultery, thus presenting fornication (as meaning premarital sexual intercourse) as being opposed to the plan and will of God.

3. In two passages Paul specifically objects to premarital sexual intercourse and recommends that normal sexual needs be met in marriage. Note: this is "specific" advice about the problems of premarital sex relations.

Youth and Self-Control

The Bible is clear in encouraging people to follow a life of strict sexual self-control. In light of the false assumption that the Bible gives no foundation for rejecting premarital relations, let us review some general passages that call for youthful self-control. In Proverbs 5:1-8, young unmarried men are instructed in strong and stern terms not to express their sexual nature through promiscuous sexual intercourse with loose women. In I Timothy 5:22, Paul urges the young man Timothy to "keep thyself pure." In II Timothy 2:22, Paul encourages Timothy "to control his turbulent and impulsive sexual desires, to give his positive attention to goodness, faith, love, and peace, and to associate with those who approach God in sincerity and with pure hearts" (a free translation).

Paul, in telling the Corinthian Christians (I Corinthians 6) that Christian liberty does not mean sexual license, says, "The body is not intended for sexual immorality but for the service of the Lord, and the Lord is for the body to serve (v. 13, *Williams).* Shun immorality . . . the immoral man sins against his own body (v. 18, RSV). Do you not

Sexual Understanding Before Marriage

know that your body is a temple of the Holy Spirit within you, which you have from God? (v. 19, RSV). So glorify God in your body" (v. 20, RSV). In discussing sexual purity with the Thessalonians (I Thessalonians 4), Paul says, "...you ought to live so as to please God (v. 1). For it is God's will that you should keep pure in person, that you should practice abstinence from sexual immorality (v. 3). For God did not call us to a life of immorality, but to one of personal purity" (v. 7, *Williams*)

In warning the Ephesian Christians about sexual vices, Paul says, "Stop letting anyone deceive you with groundless arguments about these things, for it is because of these very sins that God's anger comes upon the disobedient. So you must stop having anything to do with them. . . . You must live like children of light, for the product of light consists in practicing everything that is good and right and true; you must approve what is pleasing to the Lord. Stop having anything to do with the profitless doings of darkness; instead you must continue to expose them" (Ephesians 5:6-11, *Williams*).

Knowledge Imparted in Sexual Intercourse

Finally, the frequent use of the word "knew" in the Scriptures to describe the experience of sexual intercourse between husband and wife is further evidence that sex belongs only to marriage. The Bible indicates that sexual intercourse should be reserved for marriage because it is the divinely created plan and method to be used in initiating and continuing a "one-flesh" unity between husband and wife. Jesus assumed this when He said, "For this cause shall a man leave his father and mother, and cleave to his wife; and they twain shall be one flesh: so they are no more twain, but one flesh" (Mark 10:7, 8). The Hebrews wisely used the word "knew" in referring to the first sexual intercourse of young married people as in Genesis 4:1, "And Adam *knew* Eve his wife; and she conceived," and I Samuel

1:19, "Elkanah *knew* Hannah his wife." This language was continued in the New Testament (Matthew 1:25). The Greek word "to know" meant "to know thoroughly," "to know by experience." These passages indicate that sexual intercourse reveals a special kind of knowledge to a man about himself and about his wife. Also, it reveals a special kind of knowledge to a woman about herself and about her husband. It communicates information that cannot be described in words and cannot be received in any other way. Ernest White describes this in saying, "The mutual self-disclosure of sexual intercourse is of a nature where the individual becomes aware of the meaning of male or female. In sexual intercourse one discovers the meaning of one's own sexual existence while discovering the personal being of the other individual to which one is thus joined."[2]

In a similar manner, William Hamilton says, "In the sexual act we know what it means to be a man or a woman, and we also help the other to discover what it means to be a man or woman. We know, for the first time in a clear way, the meaning of our sexuality. . . . We know ourselves in a way we have never known another person before. . . . In this act of utter self-giving, we know ourselves as whole and fulfilled in a unique way."[3]

Thus sexual intercourse involves the inner nature and sacredness of the self, the core of the personality, the total reality of the individual. The bottomless depth and the profound significance of this experience is exceedingly intimate and truly sacred. This is the nature of sexuality as God created it. One is not surprised when White writes, ". . . knowledge that is imparted in sexual intercourse cannot be erased. Therefore, the participating individuals can never return to their former state."[4] It is, therefore, obvious that this experience was planned

[2] Ernest White, *Marriage and the Bible*, Broadman Press, 1965, p. 13.
[3] William Hamilton, *Christianity and Crisis* (October 28, 1957), p. 141.
[4] White, pp. 13-14.

to establish and promote a permanent one-flesh relationship in marriage. It does not belong to singleness. Not only is sexual intercourse designed to establish the one-flesh nature of marriage, but each sexual experience is symbolic of the complete marriage relationship, and thus it is divinely planned to sustain and secure that relationship. As William Hamilton says so aptly, "Each succeeding act of sexual intercourse through the years 'expresses utter self-giving, complete concern for the other, full willingness to grant the other the place of first importance.' " Thus "marriage is the only structure in our society that can bear all the meaning that this particular symbol conveys. Only in marriage is there the mutual dependence, the utter need of one for the other, that is acted out in the sexual act."[5]

Summary

When we consider (1) the words used, (2) the direct statements made, and (3) the general context of these words and statements, it is necessary to conclude that the Bible, with incisive clarity, calls young people (and old) to a life of uncompromising self-control, a life of sexual purity. The Hebrew-Christian point of view firmly proclaims that all those persons who abuse and misuse sex have violated the will of God (I Thessalonians 4:3), are the enemies of God (Galatians 5:19-22), have opposed the leadership of the Holy Spirit (I Thessalonians 5:23), and have characteristics like those people who are outside of the kingdom of God (Ephesians 5:5).

[5] Hamilton, p. 142.

APPENDIX II

Hebrew-Christian Ontology As Related to Sex Morals

The present struggle between the new morality and Christian ethics is, in the final analysis, a struggle between the materialistic monism of secular culture and the middle-of-the-road dualism of the New Testament, which views man as being both "non-material" and "material." The teachings of the New Testament force us to reject two extreme philosophies: Materialistic Monism and Idealistic Monism (or Subjective Idealism). They are both radical, narrow-minded, and often bigoted extremes and are directly opposed to Judeo-Christian concepts because they are based on part-truths and ignore much of reality.

When the post-New Testament church fathers reacted against the immorality of pagan polytheism, they embraced an extreme dualism after the pattern of Plato the Greek and Mani the Persian. This dualism, the opposite extreme of monism, made a sharp dichotomy between the flesh and the spirit and labeled the flesh evil and the spirit good. There is not a trace of this pagan ascetic dualism in the Hebrew or Christian thinking of either the Old or the New Testaments. It is impossible to fathom the havoc and disaster this dualism has wrought in both personal development and social relationships in human history. But, the real problem is not the fact of dualism, but the *extreme type* of dualism brought into the church from the outside by the Early Church fathers. One of the major purposes of the Protestant Reformation, when properly understood, was to reject this ascetic dualism. Since the Reformation, evangelical Protestants have continued the effort to root ascetic dualism out of Christian thought. Progress has been slow but certain. Scientific findings have greatly aided Christianity in its rejection of ascetic dualism.

Unfortunately, liberal theologians, unhappy with the progress being made in rejecting ascetic dualism, have embraced a pseudo-scientific and an extreme empirical approach in their thought and, in so doing, have moved into the welcome arms of current materialistic monism. This theological, materialistic monism, together with secular monism, has caused even greater devastation to personal and social progress than ascetic dualism ever did, if this be possible. It is this primitive materialistic monism, dressed up in the new garments of liberal theology and our derelict secular culture, that is the father of the immorality of our generation. Certainly many of these so-called church leaders who are on the outer fringe of Christian thought must shoulder much of the responsibility for the current crisis in morality.

The only possible way to bring order out of the immoral chaos of our day is to return to Biblical ontology and, therefore, to the personal, social, moral, and spiritual concepts which follow. Among other things, this must include a dualism of both the non-material and the material. Some refer to it as organic unity between physical impulses and the spiritual dimension of human personality. In discussing the nature of man, the late W. T. Conner stated that:

> The Biblical account of creation indicates that man is composed of a material and an immaterial element.... In favor of the dichotomous view it should be noted that Jesus used body and soul to include man's whole being (Matthew 10:28), also that he used soul to denote the highest and most wonderful element in man (Mark 8:36);

that the book of Revelation uses the term soul to describe disembodied martyrs (6:9).[1]

Conner has given us a fair description of the middle-of-the-road evangelical Protestant approach to the nature of man. The nature of man includes both non-material and material elements. Both work beautifully together in this earthly time existence. Neither is evil, but both may be used in evil ways by the human will. Instead of ascetic dualism, Christian ontology calls for a "fifty-one percent dualism" in which the non-material can never be less than fifty-one percent of reality and the material can never be more than forty-nine percent of reality. This allows flexibility in our understanding of human nature, yet firmly rejects suicidal extremes. This fifty-one percent dualism lays a solid foundation for a realistic understanding of the nature and purpose of sex in the human male and female.

Platonic dualism drew a sharp dichotomy between mind and matter. Christians have reacted sharply against Platonic dualism and think in terms of man as a "total person," composed of both mind and matter or flesh and spirit. Unfortunately, some materialistic liberals have carried this "total person" to such an extreme it is obvious that their "total person" refers to a monistic, biological unit.

When the materialistic philosopher objects to these two realities as being rationally impossible, we answer "so what?" It is obvious that this objection rests upon "reason" as ultimate, rather than upon reality and revelation. Christian thought must always use the processes of reason and be grateful for this God-given capacity. But reason can never be used as a god or a final guide. The limitations of reason must always be considered. Reason, like science, must always be servant — never master. Revelation and the realities of life and human experience transcend reason. When reason breaks down,

[1] W. T. Conner, *A System of Christian Doctrine*, Baptist Sunday School Board, 1924, pp. 301-302.

as it does in this case, revelation and reality must take over. Yet reason and science must continue as our efficient servants in helping man to pinpoint the nature of reality. Only then can the immoral sex crisis of our age be changed.

APPENDIX III

Some Suggestions to Churches on Sex Education[1]

Although sex education belongs to the family, solid scientific facts indicate that millions of mothers and fathers need some outside help. The churches of a community, with (1) their close ties to the family and (2) their Christian concepts concerning marriage and family life, have an ideal situation for an efficient sex education program. Although the responsibilities of pastors are legion, most pastors feel that sex education is part of the church's responsibility. This is as it should be. In some cases the pastor may want to delegate some of the leadership responsibility to his wife, his educational director, some other member of the church staff, or some other leader in the church membership such as a Christian doctor, a nurse, a social worker, or a teacher. The pastor may want to use a church "Christian Life" committee to help him lead out in the area of counseling. But if he delegates counseling responsibility, he will need to be careful to select those leaders in his church who have the proper attitude and personality. He would want to train these persons thoroughly for this important aspect of church life. The following suggestions for pastors and churches are concerned with the general sex education of youth.

[1] These suggestions are a revision of Appendix III, *Sexual Happiness in Marriage*.

1. Sex education should begin with the training of the parents of children (ages 1-8) on "how to talk to their children about sex." Once every year or two the pastor or another qualified person could lecture to a meeting of these parents. At the meeting, literature could be distributed to them. In this approach, Christianity and the church can be associated with the subject of sex in the thinking of the parents from the very beginning, and they will welcome this information.

2. The church should plan separate meetings of girls (ages 9-12) with their mothers and of boys (ages 9-12) with their fathers for a film and/or lecture on sex education. Illustrative charts could be used. These meetings should be designed to prepare the junior boys and girls for the onset of puberty. There is an advantage in having children and their parents attend this type lecture together. It will tend to promote parent-child discussion on the subject at home. Most parents will welcome this type of meeting, sponsored by the church. This lecture could be given by the pastor to the boys and by the pastor's wife or a nurse to the girls, or some other responsible church leader could be assigned this duty. Careful preparation is a *must* for those who lead these meetings. Literature and films or slides may be secured from your denominational or religious bookstores.

3. A similar meeting should be held for the teens and young people (ages 13 and up) of the church. The age division of all the above meetings could be adjusted to fit the needs of the specific church. In case of small town or rural churches, these meetings may be planned and carried out through the use of the existing organizational missionary, or some other county or divisional denominational leader could specialize in these lectures and assist smaller churches in this sex education training.

In addition to materials from your religious bookstores, churches can receive excellent literature — books and pamphlets — on sex education and family life from:

The American Institute of Family Relations
5287 Sunset Boulevard
Los Angeles, California 90027

Also, the American Institute of Family Relations publishes a monthly 12-page service bulletin, *Family Life*, $2.00 per year. *Family Life* is designed for counselors, clergymen, physicians, social workers, and other professional people who are interested in keeping abreast of development in the field of marriage and family life. It reports current research, reviews new books and pamphlets, and reports national and international news on marriage and family life. In addition to his own denominational magazines, a pastor will find *Family Life* a welcome monthly visitor to his study.

The church meetings suggested above could be made a part of a "Family Life" emphasis week or a "Christian Family Life Revival." The sermons on Sundays could be built around such subjects as "the sacredness and/or sinfulness of human personality" and "the importance of the family structure and mature sexual morality for normal community life." These Christian Family weeks could be made evangelistic. To put sex education and evangelism together would be a new approach, but skillfully and devoutly led, it could be most effective.

We cannot depend upon the county, state, and federal governments to solve the sex revolution. Permanent jobs, good food, nice houses, and plenty of money — as important as they are — can never change the immoral course of our current sex revolution. We must get at the cause of the problem — the lack of responsible parental leadership in the lives of growing children, including the area of sex education. Christian parents (assisted by the churches) must furnish the leadership. They must be the aggressors to spearhead the counterattack. They must be thorough, skillful, determined, courageous, and, above all, divinely led. To change the sexual trends in our society will take time — two or three generations; it will take patience. But it can be done. Only thus can we stabilize the family and swing the moral pendulum in the other direction — the divine direction.

APPENDIX IV

A Selected Bibliography

The following books written from a general Christian viewpoint are recommended reading in the area of sex education, courtship, marriage, and family life. These books belong in family and church libraries.

I. Practical Books on Sex Education and Morality

1. Duvall, Evelyn Millis, *Why Wait Till Marriage?* Association Press, New York, 1965.

    In *Why Wait Till Marriage?*, Dr. Duvall, queen of American sociologists and marriage and family life scholars, takes up, one by one, every argument used to justify premarital sexual relations, including such bewhiskered excuses as: "Our sex morals are old-fashioned"; "What harm can experimenting do?"; "But we're really in love!"; "It's the only way to know whether we're really right for each other." And she undermines with facts the latest fallacious rationalization: "But it's perfectly 'safe' today."

    A glance at the Table of Contents at the front of *Why Wait Till Marriage?* shows how Dr. Duvall builds chapters around such usual arguments as these, explaining by common-sense reasoning why each argument is unsound. This book is thus organized to answer specific questions, as well as to be read from beginning to end.

Parents, counselors, family life educators, and all others who live or work with young adults will find *Why Wait Till Marriage?* a unique and helpful resource.

2. Shedd, Charles W., *The Stork Is Dead.* Word Books, Publishers, Waco, Texas, 1968.

   Dr. Shedd is a nationally known clergyman. *The Stork Is Dead* grew out of a dialogue through correspondence with almost 10,000 teen-agers . . . readers of his columns in *Teen Magazine* on sex and dating. This is a frank book on sex, written for teen-agers in a language teen-agers can understand and believe. It is a valuable book, although some evangelical readers may disagree with certain of the ideas presented.

3. Kolb, Erwin J., *Parents Guide to Christian Conversation About Sex.* Concordia Publishing House, St. Louis, 1967.

   This book is one of a series of six in the Lutheran (Missouri Synod) Concordia Sex Education Series. It is written for parents to be of assistance to them in the all-important task of guiding their children in the area of sex attitudes. It gives parents specific help in talking to children on all age levels about sex, from ages three to five through high school and college.

4. *What to Tell Your Child About Sex,* prepared by the Child Study Association of America, Duell, Sloan and Pearce Publishers, New York, 1964.

II. *Books Which Present a Christian Theology of Sex*

1. Piper, Otto A., *The Biblical View of Sex and Marriage.* Charles Scribner's Sons, New York, 1960.

   This is an able and thorough discussion of the Biblical concept of marriage and sexuality. It approaches the subject in light of two basic assumptions: (1) the spiritual, social, and ethical

A Selected Bibliography

treatment of sex should start from the nature of sex and (2) Christian leaders and theologians should derive their interpretation of sex from the Bible.

2. Bailey, Derrick S., *The Mystery of Love and Marriage*. Harper and Brothers, New York, 1952.

   A scholarly Biblical study of the sexual relationship in marriage, with many helpful insights into the nature of love and permanent significance of "one flesh."

3. White, Ernest, *Marriage and the Bible*. Broadman Press, Nashville, 1965.

   This book is a comprehensive survey of Biblical teachings on marriage. It combines Biblical interpretation, theology, and psychology to present a thorough discussion of what the Bible says about marriage — and about its problems.

4. Feucht, Oscar E. (Editor), *Sex and the Church*. Concordia Publishing House, St. Louis, Missouri, 1961.

   This book is one of a series of six that has been published by The Family Life Committee of the Lutheran Church - Missouri Synod. It examines all that has been taught in the past and that which is being taught today on the subject of sex. This is a middle-of-the-road interpretation of the Bible teachings on sex. The last chapters present the contemporary views of Protestants, Roman Catholics, and Lutherans. The final chapter, "A Christian Interpretation of Sex," is one of the most practical discussions in print on Christianity and sex. This book, written by outstanding scholars, is in simple, practical language. (The other books in this series are Mate Selection, Family Authority, Divorce and Remarriage, Planned Parenthood, and Engagement and Marriage.)

5. Howell, John C., *Teachings About Sex — A*

Christian Approach. Broadman Press, Nashville, 1966.

The central theme of this book is a conviction that the home and the church share responsibility in the task of developing more wholesome Christian concepts of the meaning and expression of human sexuality. The book is specifically directed toward parents and pastors who must share the creative task of molding the attitudes of youth and adults in Christian homes and local churches.

6. Drakeford, John W., *The Great Sex Swindle.* Broadman Press, Nashville, 1966.

This provocative book points out the reasons for the change in attitude toward sexual morality, showing that they are many and interrelated. The author feels that our culture, for the most part, has misled us through its insistence on permissiveness. He points out how psychology and other social sciences have shown us that to exercise controls is better than not to exercise them.

III. *Books Which Fuse Christian Theology and Sex Techniques Necessary for Good Sexual Adjustment in Marriage*

These books may be called "Christian sex manuals."

1. Miles, Herbert J., *Sexual Happiness in Marriage.* Zondervan Publishing House, Grand Rapids, 1967.

This is a frank discussion of the role of sex in Christian marriage. It unites (1) a Christian and Biblical theology of sex, (2) sociological research, and (3) the detailed techniques necessary for good sexual adjustment in marriage into a Christian sex manual. It is written to be read by engaged couples and married couples. Such chapters as

(1) The Reproductive and Sexual Organs,

(2) Basic Methods in Sexual Adjustment in Marriage,

(3) The Honeymoon: First Sexual Experiences,

(4) Controlling Parenthood Through the Use of Contraceptives, and

(5) Poor Sexual Adjustment in Marriage

are written in careful detail, yet in Christian dignity and without offense.

2. Fritze, Julius A., *The Essence of Marriage*. Zondervan Publishing House, Grand Rapids, 1969.

Rev. Julius A. Fritze is a Lutheran clergyman, a practicing clinical psychologist and marriage counselor. This book has been written in answer to the cries for help that he has heard in many years of experience as a marriage counselor. It unites theology, psychology, and the human sciences. He finds no conflict between scientific facts and Biblical teachings on sexuality in marriage. Some of the chapter headings are:

What Is Love and What Is Marriage?

Maturity and Compatibility

Psychological Differences Between Men and Women

The Art of Communication

Sex Life in Marriage

In-laws

For a fuller discussion of the nature and functions of male and female sexual organs see *Human Sexual Response* (1966) and *Human Sexual Inadequacy* (1970) by Masters and Johnson, Little, Brown and Co. Also, see *Sex Without Fear* by Lewin and Gilmore, Medical Research Press, New York, 1962.